What Are They Saying About the Social Setting of the New Testament?

REVISED AND EXPANDED EDITION

Carolyn Osiek, RSCJ

PAULIST PRESS
New York/Mahwah

Osiek, Carolyn.
    What are they saying about the social setting of the New
Testament? / Carolyn Osiek. — Rev. ed.
        p. cm.
    Includes bibliographical references.
    ISBN 0-8091-3339-3
    1. Sociology, Biblical.   2. Bible.   N.T.—Criticism,
interpretation, etc.   I. Title.
    BS2545.S55065   1992
    225.6'7—dc20   92-16470
                                                                        CIP

Published by Paulist Press
997 Macarthur Blvd. Mahwah, N.J. 07430

Printed and bound in the
United States of America

Contents

PART IV: USING SOCIAL SCIENCE MODELS

*To My Parents,
My First and Lasting Models
of Christian Community*

Introduction

A New Field of Biblical Inquiry

For some years now experts in the social sciences have been turning their attention to one of the richest fields for the study of human group interaction: religion. Similarly, classicists and ancient historians have been investigating for over a century the history, economy, literature, and social life of the Greek and Roman civilizations that flourished on the shores of the Mediterranean Sea in the centuries just before and after the beginning of the Christian era. Meanwhile, back in the church, theologians and biblicists have been pondering even longer that collection of writings which Jews and Christians hold to be divinely inspired: the Bible. With few exceptions, the three groups continued on their respective ways with little to say to one another.

What has happened in recent years, however, has changed the picture. Scholars in the three fields are now listening to one another more, so that the methods and findings of the social scientists and the researchers of Greco-Roman civilization can be brought to bear on the Bible and, more specifically for our present interest, on the New Testament and the beginnings of the church.

Underlying this new trend in biblical studies is an important assumption. The church is both divine and human; the Bible is both word of God and human word. As God's word, it transcends history and culture, as does the church in its transcendent aspect. But as human word, the Bible is produced by a human church, subject to the historical vision and cultural patterns of the faith communities and writers which produced it.

1

The more we realize this last assertion and its implications, the more we are aware of the problems it poses. It means that we must always leave open the possibility, often to the point of probability, that a biblical statement comes out of a certain historical and cultural perspective which may or may not be ours.

Between the first and the twentieth centuries there is not only a tremendous expanse of time. The scientific and psychological revolutions that have taken place in the last five hundred years have irreversibly changed the way we (at least we westerners and those others touched in some way by western culture) see the world and interpret experience. When I watch the sun move across the sky, I see a fiery ball, the center of our universe, around which our planet revolves. I do not see a golden orb passing through the extended body of the sky goddess Nut as did the ancient Egyptians, or Apollo's golden chariot traveling across the sky as did the Greeks. If I have the misfortune to experience an earthquake, I attribute it to geological disturbances beneath the earth's surface, not to the anger of the god of the underworld. And if I suddenly begin engaging in violent anti-social behavior, I will be confined for psychiatric evaluation, not exorcism, before any judgment is made about responsibility and penalty for my actions.

These simple examples serve to illustrate a complex fact, that we moderns have a totally different way of constructing and interpreting our world than did people of ancient times. So when we translate and interpret the Bible, we necessarily do it in our own terms, in words and concepts familiar to us from our own cultural world. This realization must make us think at least twice before saying that we know with absolute certainty what a biblical passage means.

Does this mean that there is no timeless truth in the Bible, that everything in it is merely cultural conditioning? No, it does not. Because the Bible is God's word, it does contain timeless truth. This truth is expressed *through* the human word, so that the attempt to understand its meaning (exegesis) must always take into account what a text *meant* in its own historical, social, and literary context as well as what it *means* today in ours. To neglect either step is to interpret very inadequately. The social and sociological study of early Christianity can help enormously with the first of these steps. (The difference between social and sociological will be explained below.)

How Did We Get There from Form Criticism?

Those who have followed the evolution of New Testament studies in the last century, or who have even had a good New Testament course in college or graduate school, know that the so-called "historical-critical method," pioneered by Martin Dibelius and Rudolf Bultmann in the early years of this century, has dominated New Testament study. Form criticism seeks to identify literary forms in the text; source criticism isolates literary and oral sources upon which the author has drawn; redaction criticism attends to how the author has worked with his material in order to make his own theological points; historical criticism leads to judgments about the historical reliability of information contained in a text. All of these helpful exercises lead toward one goal: establishing as nearly as possible what the text meant in its own environment.

Now there is the feeling among many scholars that, while these methods are just beginning to be applied to much of the non-canonical literature surrounding both Old and New Testaments, their possibilities have just about been exhausted in regard to the New Testament, and that to gain new insights we need to look at the text through different eyes. Another factor is the increase of social awareness and concern on the part of the churches, prompting questions about such issues as the economic background of Jesus and the first Christians, their attitudes about family life, the poor, the role of women, etc.

This recent concern about the social framework of the New Testament has earlier precedents in the work of such writers as those of the "Chicago School," Shirley Jackson Case (*Evolution of Early Christianity,* 1914; *The Social Origins of Christianity,* 1923; *The Social Triumph of the Ancient Church,* 1934) and Shailer Matthews (*The Social Teaching of Jesus: An Essay in Christian Sociology,* 1897; *The Atonement and the Social Process,* 1930). Frederick Grant's *Economic Background of the Gospels* (first published 1926; republished N.Y.: Atheneum, 1973) was equally influential and of lasting value. But studies like these were not frequent, and were produced under the influence of this century's first wave of American Christian social concern, which gave way in the 1930s to more dogmatic and ecclesiological pursuits.

Now within the past ten years or so an increasing number of books and articles have appeared on the social context and structure of early Christianity. They hold promise of being the beginning of a new direction in New Testament studies, providing methods which can be used alongside the historical-critical methods to yield fresh insights about the biblical texts and the people who wrote and first read them.

Social and Sociological

Actually we are dealing not with one approach but two, and it is well at this point to make the distinction which is too often blurred even by scholars in the field.

On the one hand, there is social description and analysis, using the findings of archaeology (excavations, art, inscriptions, coins), history, and literature contemporary to the texts. Through this method we can gather data and form concepts regarding social life and organization, political life, institutions, social dynamics, and horizons of consciousness. For example, a solid acquaintance with customs of pagan temple sacrifice and the social institution of private banquets in first century Corinth can shed quite a bit of light on Paul's discussion of eating meat offered to idols in 1 Corinthians 8:1–13 and 10:14–33. Again, an investigation of official language of the Roman emperor cult through literary texts, inscriptions, and coins suggests that the readers of Luke 2:10–11 would have read far more political overtones into those simple lines than we do.

On the other hand, the application of social science theory to New Testament texts is quite another thing. This method obviously builds on the other, for without adequate detailed information a sociological analysis would be impossible. Here the constructs of sociologists and cultural or social anthropologists like Max Weber,[1] Ernst Troeltsch,[2] Mary Douglas,[3] Peter Berger,[4] Victor Turner[5] and many others have proved especially helpful to New Testament scholars. Thus for instance Weber's theories about the evolution of a sect into an institution and the consequent changes in the notion of charism have provided one way of interpreting the characteristics of the Pauline churches and the way community structures and "charismatic" gifts seem to be treated differently between the earlier and later letters of the Pauline collection. Or again, Turner's categories of "structure" and "communitas," like Douglas' slightly different "group" and "grid" as complementary poles of individual and communal self-awareness, provide a framework for looking in a new way at the formation of Christian identity and community in the early church.

The study of the New Testament and early Christianity with social science models presents some serious difficulties. Foremost among them is the obvious fact that social science theories are modern constructions whose users can sometimes forget about the time gap of which we have spoken between us and first century people, and assume in subtle and not so subtle ways that our concepts and theirs are the same. This is where a wise use of social or cultural (British and American terms nearly identical in meaning) anthropology saves the day, for anthropology by its nature is cross-cultural and comparative, and therefore less vulnerable to this pitfall. Another difficulty is that texts from the New Testament and other ancient literature were not written with the purpose of yielding the kind of information which the sociologist primarily seeks: 1 Corinthians was not written as a social description of the Corinthian community but as a pastoral commentary on theological and disciplinary problems; the gospel of John was not written to describe the relationship of Johannine Christians to the rest of the world but to make strong and uncompromising statements about the identity of Jesus as believed by that community. Yet in both cases, to cite only these two examples, the reader on the lookout for sociological clues must seek them in the texts and whatever other literary or archaeological evidence is available, for that is all we have. We must realize that we are working with incomplete evidence.

Still another difficulty is that in the case of biblical texts we are dealing with literature that is not only social but also theological, not only historical but also canonical, that is, authoritative in some way. Theology is one of the most effective ways of structuring life and of giving meaning to experience. In that sense it is matter for sociological analysis. But theology of its nature transcends the social plane and provides means of experiencing that which is beyond what can be perceived and conceived. Thus there is a fear that a sociological study of the New Testament will reduce religious experience to patterns of group behavior to be observed and categorized, rather than recognizing it as a bridge between everyday existence and transcendence. But any method applied too narrowly will be reductionistic; theology out of contact with social reality can be just as narrow. The problem of reductionism lies not in a method but in how that method is used.

In spite of the potential difficulties which must be constantly kept in mind by scholars using these methods, the social and social science approaches to the New Testament and early Christianity are providing new and valid insights into the life and experience of the first Christians, and, even more important, into how we can today better understand and live their faith.

The following pages are an attempt to summarize some of the principal approaches and discoveries of the social and sociological study of the New Testament. Because this is a rapidly expanding new body of literature, it is impossible to discuss or even mention everything that has been written in the area. Since the first edition of this book in 1984, methods have been refined and numerous new books and articles have appeared. For more detailed and evaluative accounts, see some of the summary articles and books that have been published.[6]

> Those of you who have been baptized into Christ
> have put on Christ.
> There is no Jew nor Greek,
> there is no slave nor free,
> there is no male and female,
> for you are all one in Christ Jesus (Gal 3:27–28).

Paul's proclamation of baptismal unity claims to overcome the differences of race, status, and sex which human society imposes. Baptism into the Christian community overcomes these barriers proleptically—that is, we begin in our own history to catch a glimpse of future possibilities. We cannot see the full realization now, but we can look forward to it, and meanwhile seek to implement the vision in our own lives.

Here I am reminded of Mary Daly's statement of many years ago: "In Christ there is neither male nor female. The trouble is, everywhere else there *is!*" What can be said of sexual discrimination can be said as well of race and social status. The baptismal statement used by Paul in the above passage cuts to the heart of differences and divisions in human society. As has always been the case, the people of the New Testament brought their own cultural experience with its patterns of perception and behavior with them into the church. As Christians they continued to see the world as people of their own time. It is this world of the first century Mediterranean culture that we will now explore.

Part I
JEW AND GREEK:
MERGING CULTURES

1
Judaism and Hellenism
in the First Century

It is not the purpose of this volume to give an account of historical events. For historical accounts the reader is referred to the appropriate sections in books on New Testament background, of which there are many, or to F.F. Bruce, *New Testament History* or Bo Reicke, *The New Testament Era,* whole volumes devoted to the history of the period just before and after the time of New Testament events. What will be discussed here are recent findings with regard to social and cultural interaction during that time.

We are speaking here of "Judaism" and "Hellenism." Most readers will be reasonably sure they know what is meant by Judaism: a religious tradition and cultural grouping existing from ancient times, historically connected with the land of Palestine, and characterized by a strong monotheistic faith based on that part of the Bible which Christians are accustomed to call the Old Testament. With that broad a definition probably any Jewish groups in the ancient world would have agreed, but the varieties of Jewish religion and culture in the Roman empire were equally as varied as they are today. A Pharisee in Jerusalem and a philosophical writer in the diaspora like Philo of Alexandria may have had very little in common in regard to lifestyle, piety, or interpretation of the scriptures. What they would have uncompromisingly agreed upon, however, is the legacy of those scriptures to testify to God's continuing covenant with Israel.

Our second term, "Hellenism," may need more explanation. The classical Greek culture of earlier centuries was taking on new forms in the late fourth century BCE, just at the time of a movement that was to change the face of the eastern Mediterranean world. The Macedonians in the northern mountains of Greece under the leadership of Alexander the Great began a military expansion to the east to subdue the Persian empire and open the way to India. In their wake came Greek, or Hellenistic, culture. When Alexander died suddenly in Persia at the height of his career in 323 BCE, his generals divided up the eastern Mediterranean from Greece all the way to Egypt into empires for themselves, Greek empires in which government, economics, and culture were syncretized into a new kind of civilization that was to be adapted later by the Romans and remain the dominant culture in the eastern Mediterranean world until the Arab conquest of the seventh century.

In Palestine and in diaspora Jewish communities elsewhere, Jewish and Hellenistic culture came into direct contact and in some cases conflict. When two cultures meet, elements of each are retained, dropped, or transformed. This kind of phenomenon has been continually studied by sociologists and anthropologists and is continually occurring. One need only remember the "melting pot" of nineteenth century American immigration or observe what is happening today with new waves of immigrants. In the case of the immigrants, the challenge is adapting to a local dominant culture into which they are plunged. To better understand the analogy to the ancient world and Hellenism, we need to observe how the resident or local culture is affected by the new arrivals: the influence of African music on jazz, the necessity for bilingualism in southern Florida or California, etc.

The older cultures of the ancient Near East, that of the Jews in Palestine among them, were now beset with invader-conquerors who brought their own language, dress, lifestyle, religion, government, taxation systems, and manufactured products, and proceeded to impose them on the local population. First experienced in its economic and political effects, Hellenism became within a century the culture of the upper classes in the whole eastern Mediterranean.

After military occupation came civil government structures

with their particularly hated aspect of taxation, administered by the method that remained in force through Roman times: tax farming—government concession of the right to collect taxes within a given area. Whether property taxes, poll taxes, sales or road use taxes, all were generally collected by agents hated not only for their immediate role, but also as representatives of a foreign occupying power except in Palestine from about 134 to 64 BCE during the Jewish Hasmonean monarchy.

More subtle Greek influence followed. Many of the Jerusalem aristocracy realized that under this regime the only way to prosper was to adopt certain aspects of Greek culture: language, dress, participation in the leisure activities of theater and athletics, assuming Greek names and giving them to their children. Some of this is described in 1 Maccabees 1:11–15 and 2 Maccabees 4:10–15 through events of about 170 BCE, especially the aristocracy building a gymnasium and sending their sons to compete in athletic contests, even going to the point of undergoing plastic surgery to remove the sign of circumcision so they would not be ridiculed by their Greek companions. Notice that in both accounts it is Jews, not foreigners, who initiate these cultural adaptations. In this case they are not being imposed upon directly by their pagan occupiers.

This is not to say that there was no pressure to conform. Cultured Greeks of the period tended to see themselves as racially and culturally superior to "barbarians" (everyone else), who then felt it necessary to prove themselves by demonstrating how Greek they could be.

To stricter Jews, however, these kinds of changes meant compromise and apostasy from the Jewish faith, for it was impossible to live like a Greek and observe the law in its full rigor, just as it was virtually impossible to frequent theater, baths, and gymnasium without being associated with Greek religion in the form of public prayer and sacrifice. Moreover, the exposure of the body required for bathing at the public baths and competing nude at the gymnasium was considered morally reprehensible. During the first century of Greek rule under the Ptolemies of Egypt, there was less pressure, less direct interference in local affairs in Palestine. But after the country was taken over by a rival dynasty, the Seleucids from Antioch about 200 BCE, more direct policies of Hellenization were pursued. It was the clash between this and the older culture in Palestine, and specifically the intended "reform" by the "enlightened" Hellenized Jerusalem artistocrats, encouraged and sanctioned by the rather naive Seleucid king Antiochus Epiphanes, which provoked the Maccabean revolt of the 160s BCE, the story of which is narrated in 1 and 2 Maccabees.

The Maccabean war was the beginning of the reestablishment of home rule under the Hasmonean dynasty until that monarchy was usurped by Herod the Great in 40 BCE. But rather than being the end of Hellenism, it was the beginning. The Hasmoneans continued to be quite influenced by it in culture, if not in religion. Historical and archaeological evidence, some only recently brought to light, indicates that Herod's remodeling of Jerusalem and the temple turned them into magnificent showplaces in Greco-Roman style, so that the Jerusalem Jesus knew was not that of today's Old City with its narrow winding medieval streets, but a city in stone and marble with a sixty foot wide main street and graceful columned porticoes. Herod was also responsible for the splendid new seaport of Caesarea on the coast, later seat of Roman administration, an entirely new Roman city which was to be a significant location for both Peter (Acts 10) and Paul (Acts 23:23—26:23).[1]

Most of this information has been known all along, of course, for it is part of the biblical literature and the *Antiquities* of the first century historian Josephus. It has been customary to look at the clash between Judaism and Hellenism in Palestine in the Hellenistic period as simply one of two cultures, that of the conquered and that of the conquerors, with a minimum of intermingling and a great deal of resistance on the part of the conquered.

In view of more careful study of the literature and archaeological evidence and some comparative study of other similar situations, several new approaches have come to light.

It is too simple to see this encounter as that of two competing cultures, but we can understand its dynamics much better if we can see it in terms of tradition and modernity. Some people collect antiques, others collect video games. Typically, the older generation generally prefers to do things "the way they've always been done," whether in communications, interior decoration, shopping, entertainment, or that last bastion of permanence—religion. Just as typically, the younger generation is generally more open to change because they haven't yet become familiar with definite ways of circumscribing culture.

Those who want to get ahead economically and socially will migrate to the occupations and social circles where they think this is possible—computer science, the sun belt jet set, etc. Those optimistic about progress see unlimited possibilities for the future. Those concerned about tradition and its values wonder if progress isn't betrayal. In a technological age, can science, the new religion, preserve the respect for human and family life upon which our civilization is built? Can progress and truth co exist?

To broaden the picture a bit, let us consider today's Middle East, a region as wrenched by conflict today as it was twenty centuries ago. For the strictly observant Moslem or Jew, tradition means fidelity to ancestral faith as it has been conveyed within a cultural context, including in both cases certain ways of dressing, public behavior, restriction of women to household roles, etc. But to advance socially and economically, today's Jewish or Moslem young adult must learn English, and with knowledge of the language comes exposure to a whole new world of consumerism and values alien to the traditional way of life and belief. Dressing modernly seems immodest, the sensual bombardment of the media creates different ways of relating, public roles for women are seen as a threat to the sacredness of the family and its values. Can the strength of tradition be retained if the new ways are adopted? The popularity of conservative movements both in Orthodox Israeli Judaism and in the Moslem countries is clearly saying that for many, including the young, the answer is a resounding *no*.

These are questions very similar to those asked by the sincerely religious Palestinian Jew of the mid-second century BCE. And what is important for our interests, the same questions were still being asked by the contemporaries of Jesus and Paul.

Palestinian and Hellenistic Judaism

Another new approach concerns the difference between so-called Palestinian Judaism and Hellenistic Judaism. By New Testament times there had been considerable colonies of Jews outside Palestine for at least six hundred years, particularly in Egypt and Babylonia. These diaspora Jews in the Mediterranean area found themselves after Alexander's conquest living in an increasingly Hellenized environment without the support of home city, temple, and majority population enjoyed by the Jews of Palestine. In the urban centers of Egypt, North Africa, Syria, and Asia Minor, they found themselves in a Greek world to which they more readily adapted. It was in Egypt at least by the third century BCE that the Hebrew scriptures were translated into Greek, presumably because not all in the congregation understood Hebrew. Diaspora Jews began quite early to give Greek names to their children and generally assimilate themselves as much as possible to their environment while at the same time remaining faithful to the religion of Moses and Abraham.

It had been customary for scholars to assume that Palestinian Judaism remained somehow less tainted with Hellenism, while diaspora Judaism alone could properly be called Hellenistic. Recently the thorough and monumental research of Martin Hengel has established a different picture. In his two-volume work, *Judaism and Hellenism,* followed later by the smaller *Jews, Greeks, and Barbarians,* and *The "Hellenization" of Judaea in the First Centuries after Christ,* Hengel has persuasively shown through painstaking examination of literary, archaeological, and inscriptional evidence that from as early as the middle of the third century BCE, a meaningful distinction cannot be made between Palestinian and Hellenistic Judaism. Rather, Hellenism had already by that time so pervaded daily life that Palestinian Jews differed little from their brothers and sisters in the diaspora in their outlook and the effects of Greek economic, administrative, and cultural influence in their lives, even if their native language was not Greek. Instead of distinguishing between Palestinian and Hellenistic (diaspora) Judaism, Hengel maintains, we can make a distinction between the Greek-*speaking* Judaism of the diaspora west of Palestine, and the Aramaic/Hebrew-*speaking* Judaism of Palestine and Babylonia. All of it is profoundly influenced by Greek civilization and culture, even in unacknowledged ways.

Thus, for instance, the Wisdom literary tradition, already on the way toward philosophical meditation in such books as Job and Proverbs, found familiar ground in Hellenistic literature, particularly popular Stoicism. By equating Wisdom with Torah, the law (see Ps 119), both as way of life and personified guide (see Prv 8—9; Sir 24), the Jewish Wisdom tradition was able to maintain credibility in cultured circles among admirers of Greek philosophical writings. Books like Qoheleth (Ecclesiastes) and Ben Sira (Ecclesiasticus), though very different, are examples.[2] The exact nature of Greek philosophical influence on Jewish Wisdom literature has always been impossible to make precise, but it is generally accepted that well before the writing of the New Testament, the process had already taken shape.

Less conscious borrowers, but borrowers all the same, Hengel suggests, are the Essenes, the separatist group responsible for the Dead Sea Scrolls at their Qumran monastery. Going with an already recognized theory of their origins in about 150 BCE in reaction to temple policies with which they were in disagreement, he suggests that their strict and communitarian organization and their totally confident claim to be the only legitimate representatives of authentic Judaism are matched only by the much earlier conventicles of Pythagorean philosophers, known for their asceticism and communal adherence.

Moreover, the external forms and organization of the community closely resemble those of Hellenistic private religious associations, a type of organization apparently unknown previously in Judaism. While wisely rejecting suggestions by earlier scholars of direct borrowing of Hellenistic forms of religious organization by the Jewish purist Essenes, Hengel maintains that without realizing it, and against their best intentions, even the Essenes were caught up on at least the fringes of the Hellenistic cloak.[3]

In spite of his sweeping statements about the overall effects of Hellenism in Palestine, Hengel is careful to say that he is speaking mostly of the aristocratic classes of Jerusalem when considering the greatest influence of Greek language, literature, and leisure. Unfortunately it is the leisured urban classes throughout the ancient world which left the best records of themselves, for it was they who had the education, time, and money to do so. In the areas of trade, taxation, and government, however, the effects of Hellenism were all-pervasive.

Galilee

For some perspectives on what was happening elsewhere than in Jerusalem, we must turn to the second recent major study of Palestine, Sean Freyne's *Galilee from Alexander the Great to Hadrian, 323 B.C.E. to 135 C.E.* It too has been well received by scholars in the field. In contrast to the sophisticated urban environment described by Hengel, Freyne pulls together all the evidence available from literary and archaeological sources to portray quite a different picture in the upper regions of Palestine than in the south.

Freyne challenges the interpretation of Isaiah 8:23 (or 9:1), "Galilee of the Gentiles," as indicating that in the post-exilic period there was heavy Gentile settlement in Galilee, creating a quite mixed population. Rather, after examining all the evidence available, he concludes that in the Hellenistic period and into Roman (New Testament) times, Galilee remained a largely Jewish peasant society, with most of the population residing in rural areas and villages.

Even the two major urban centers, Sepphoris in the central plain and Tiberias on the west coast of the Lake of Gennesaret, remained according to Freyne primarily Jewish, though more Hellenized in culture than the rural areas and including Gentile, mostly Greek, minorities. Similarly, the nearby Greek cities of the Decapolis, mostly on the east side of the Jordan, probably had Jewish minorities.

Sepphoris and Tiberias were both new cities in New Testament times, rebuilt in one case and built anew (over a cemetery!) in the other, both by Herod Antipas, the Herod of the gospel passion narratives. Both were administrative capitals at one time and stood in some rivalry with one another. While Sepphoris is no longer inhabited, the modern city of Tiberias gives one something of the impression that the ancient city must have conveyed, built near a hot springs spa, sprawling down the hills to the lake at its feet, visible from any point on the lake—a vacation spot in a splendid location. The excavations at Sepphoris, still in progress, may eventually help determine its degree of Hellenization in the first century. Because Tiberias is still inhabited, excavation possibilities are severely limited.

The cities had a Greek form of city government, a Greek way of life, and were therefore treated with some hostility by the rural population. Significantly, the gospels never indicate that Jesus even entered either one. In the revolt against Rome, 66–70 CE, Sepphoris remained loyal to Rome, true to its Hellenizing tendencies, while Tiberias entered the war half-heartedly, with a populace very divided on the question. It was subdued by the Roman general Vespasian, but treated not unkindly by the Roman conquerors.[4]

The Galilean towns of which we hear in the gospels—Nazareth, Bethsaida, Capernaum, Magdala, Cana, and Chorazim—were probably villages in comparison, though Bethsaida, Capernaum, and Magdala all lay along the principal road from the Mediterranean to Damascus in Roman times, and must therefore have done a brisk business in trade and supplies. Magdala (Aramaic for "tower") had an alternate name not mentioned in the gospels, Taricheae (Greek for "salted fish"), perhaps an indication of the base of its lakeside economy.

While small ancestral peasant holdings were still the basis of land allotment in Galilee in New Testament times, increasingly the best land was held in royal estates, parcelled out to whomever the prevailing occupiers wished to reward, confiscated and reallotted when its owners fell out of favor with the crown. Thus large stretches of land worked by tenant farmers were owned and administered from the urban centers, whence came also the tax farmers. The country people of Galilee experienced the effects of Hellenization in ways that did not make them well disposed to its benefits. They retained a firm and abiding loyalty to the spiritual significance of Jerusalem with its temple worship, and held more in common with the older, traditional way of life inasmuch as it could still be found in Jerusalem, than with the cities closer to them. The peasants of Galilee must have been the backbone of the traditional pilgrimages to Jerusalem for the great feasts (cf. Lk 2:41; Jn 2:23; 5:1; 7:2,10; 11:55).

What languages were spoken in Palestine at the time of Jesus? After half a century of Roman occupation, the legal language was Latin, but since apparently so few really understood it, most official documents and decrees were also promulgated in Greek. After three centuries of Hellenistic administration and commerce, the commercial language was predominantly Greek. Even most of the country people must have understood at least business and "tourist" Greek. Consider Jesus' numerous encounters with non-Jews in the gospels, from the citizens of the Greek Decapolis city Gadara or Gerasa (Mt 8:28–34; Mk 5:1–20; Lk 8:26–39) to the Roman governor Pilate in the passion narratives. Freyne rightly raises the question whether language of itself changes thought patterns, even if there is a concerted effort to prevent it. But since the Persian conquest of the sixth century BCE, Aramaic had replaced Hebrew as the everyday language of the ordinary people, and it probably remained so in rural areas and among the lower classes of the cities as well. Those who attended temple or synagogue services in Palestine, except for "Hellenist" synagogues in Jerusalem for diaspora visitors and immigrants (Acts 6:1; 9:29), heard the scripture reading in Hebrew, and could perhaps even speak it somewhat for formal occasions.[5]

In Palestine during New Testament times, then, the large cities represented centers of Greco-Roman culture and at the same time political and economic power. Jerusalem, Caesarea, Tiberias, and Sepphoris were modern centers of progress where communication with and recognition from the larger world of the Roman empire were highly valued. Here the still predominantly Jewish populations saw less difficulty combining Greek speech, dress, and lifestyle with their ancestral religious traditions than did many of their fellow Jews of the villages and countryside who were, quite simply, far less likely to benefit from Hellenism and more likely to be oppressed by it because of the prevailing economic and social system.

The Diaspora

What can be said of Jewish Hellenization in the diaspora? This is an immense topic covering a much larger range chronologically, geographically, and demographically, and could never be covered in a single study. Hengel's second work on the topic, *Jews, Greeks, and Barbarians,* gives a brief but solid introduction.[6] In areas where there were large Jewish communities and where sufficient evidence remains, we see a number of different trends happening. Jewish diaspora communities were usually cohesively organized around synagogue groupings that may have been based on neighborhood or national origin or both, sometimes with an overall *gerousia* or council of elders, for the entire Jewish population of the city, as in Alexandria. In this way they modeled their group identity as a *politeuma* or assembly of citizens within a city on the larger identity of the Greek citizens of the city as a whole. They were a city within a city. When the Jewish population of a city grew very large as in Alexandria (a third of the population in the first and second centuries CE) this could cause friction which would result in discrimination, oppression, and revolt, as indeed it did there several times during that period.

As could be expected, Jewish communities in Greek-speaking environments inevitably assimilated to Hellenistic culture, and apparently with much less strain than in Palestine. One of the obvious signs is adoption of Greek and later Latin names, just as in the somewhat later evidence of the Jews of Rome, known through funerary inscriptions, the same trend can be traced from one generation to the next, moving not from Jewish to Greek but now from Greek to Latin names.[7] Other indications include use of the Greek Bible, and the increasing influence of Greek literary and philosophical traditions on Jewish writers, especially the great philosopher Philo of Alexandria, a contemporary of Paul.[8] This assimilation happened generally in one direction only, toward Hellenism, rather than toward the older native cultures, Egyptians in Alexandria, Syrians in Antioch, etc. It followed the pattern usually found in situations where a new, modern, dominant culture points the way toward social advancement. The older cultures often get their revenge, however, particularly through influence on popular religion, magic, and superstition.

Thus another trend is also observable especially in diaspora communities: the attraction of non-Jews to certain aspects of Jewish religion, especially its strict monotheism and strong ethical standards, so that in many urban areas a steady stream of non-Jews, including Greeks and Romans, became attracted to synagogue worship and eventually attached themselves to the Jewish community, either as proselytes who took upon themselves full observance of the law (see Acts 13:43), or as interested frequenters who maintained a looser relationship. It is probably this latter group who are referred to in Acts 13:50; 16:14; 17:4,17; 18:7, though it is disputed whether "God-fearers" is a technical synagogue term or not. In the late first century something of a public scandal was created in Rome when several members of one of the best aristocratic families closely connected to the emperor Domitian himself were accused of adopting Jewish customs. Two hundred years later the church historian Eusebius claimed that they were really Christians; they may have been converts to a still quite Jewish form of Christianity, which we know continued for several centuries.

Conclusion and Implications for the New Testament

Recent investigation of the meeting of Jewish and Hellenistic culture in the formative centuries before the New Testament era has shown that in Palestine as in the diaspora, at a very early stage the urban Jews were deeply affected by Hellenism, so that the conventional distinction between Palestinian and Hellenistic (diaspora) Judaism is no longer viable.

In Palestine Greek culture was experienced at the beginning of the Hellenistic period just after the conquest by Alexander the Great first in its military, political, and economic effects. The introduction of Hellenistic systems of administration and taxation deepened the rift between urban aristocratic landholders and tax farmers on one side who stood to benefit by increasing involvement in the Hellenistic world, and the rural peasantry who were largely its victims on the other. Hellenism, always an urban culture, rewarded the upwardly-mobile city dweller at the expense of the rural population who therefore remained more loyal to traditional ways of life. These tendencies were true throughout the Greek east, not only in Palestine.

In the diaspora, Jewish communities attained a remarkable amount of cohesiveness in some of the large cities, while their assimilation to Hellenism went more smoothly in most cases. Synagogues were for the most part open centers of worship which attracted non-Jews.

In the first part of the Hellenistic era, Greek purism from earlier years remained a source of at least an ideological division between those of Greek birth, language, and culture, and the rest of humanity, grouped together uncritically as barbarians. In the early years of Roman expansion, even the Romans were considered barbarians by the Greek literary aristocracy.

There were challenges to this view, however. Already Alexander saw himself as creator of a cosmopolis, a world-city. In the first and second centuries BCE, more change of perspective was brought about under the influence of the Stoic philosophers' concept of the world community, a common human unity, brought together of course by a common language and culture, that of Hellenism.[9] While Greek culture was clearly superior, now presumably everyone could aspire to it. It was this philosophical movement toward a human community as well as the common economic and social community created by the expansion of Hellenistic power and culture in the eastern Mediterranean which facilitated Roman imperial expansion in the first century BCE and ultimately the rapid spread of Christianity in the following centuries, for it was into this world of Hellenistic urban culture that Paul and his fellow missionaries went forth to proclaim the gospel.

At this point Paul's proclamation in Galatians 3:28 and Romans 10:12 (but see the puzzling variation in Colossians 3:11) that there is neither Jew nor Greek in Christ must mean far more in light of what we have seen in the preceding pages. It should be clear by now that all of these events carry tremendous implications for our reading of the New Testament. If we are to understand its message within the context of the writers' own world, we must know something of that world, which these pages have attempted to sketch.

One important result is that we cannot facilely try to divide what is "Greek" from what is "Jewish" in New Testament literature, as writers sometimes enjoy doing. To use an example: in the prologue of John's gospel, Jesus is spoken of as the Word, or Logos in Greek. Much ink has been spilled trying to decide whether John's use of the concept comes from Greek Stoic philosophy *or*

Jewish Wisdom literature. The answer in light of recent scholarship on Hellenism and Judaism is: both together. Or again, the question arises whether the first generation of Christians in urban centers like Antioch and Corinth understood the eucharist along the model of Jewish table fellowship meals *or* Hellenistic banquets. Again, the answer has to be some of both.

Another factor to bear in mind is the difference between rural and urban life in the eastern Mediterranean, even to the point of hostility in some cases. This is a point acknowledged but not sufficiently developed by Hengel in his vigorous assertions about the extent of Hellenism in Palestine. It receives more attention from Freyne, but his focus is on Galilee, so that the rural-urban tension in Judea and other parts of Palestine has not really been studied. While Jesus and most of his followers came from Galilean village life, Matthew/Levi the tax collector may have represented an entirely different constituency, and the seven appointed to assist the apostles (Acts 6) in the early Jerusalem years are all men with Greek names serving in large part Greek-speaking Jewish Christians. The rural Palestinian roots of Christianity sprang quickly into an urban thicket. But more of this in chapter 2.

2
First Century Consciousness

Now that we have considered some of the social factors in the first century Mediterranean world in their historical setting, it will be enlightening to approach that world from another angle, that of models from the social sciences.

As mentioned earlier, we in the twentieth century west live in an entirely different world of meaning than did the people of the New Testament. The point of difference began to widen sharply in the modern era with new inventions that revolutionized communications (the printing press), warfare (gunpowder), and travel (the steam engine). Enlightenment philosophy probed the value of individualism. Modern technology creates for us a world of virtually unlimited knowledge, storage and retrieval of information, and even (some would say) unlimited economic growth.

The democratic and capitalist principles teach us that at least theoretically the individual's right to "life, liberty, and the pursuit of happiness" is supreme, that independence and self-reliance are praiseworthy, and that the possibility of advancement resulting from hard work is limitless (though it is precisely disillusionment with these lofty promises that is causing much of today's social upheaval). The psychological revolution begun by Freud's and Jung's adventures into the previously uncharted unconscious reveals to us another frontier whose limit has yet to be sighted. In short, apart from occasional setbacks and the threat of nuclear disaster, the assumptions on which our society operates are those of limitless horizons and the value of the individual over against

society. The imposing of limits, whether by economic policy, legisla-
tion, or unequal opportunity, is precisely what provokes rebellion
of one kind or another.

The sociologist or anthropologist and the biblical scholar are
together vividly aware of one major reality: we cannot go back.
There is no way that we as twentieth century westerners can completely shed our assumptions and horizon of experience and take
on the mindset of a person who has had no exposure to our culture. This of course poses a serious problem for our understanding
of the Bible, as we already saw in the introduction. What we can
do, however, is to make use of the comparative models provided
by the social sciences, in this case cultural anthropology which
studies patterns of social behavior across many cultures.

Bruce J. Malina has admirably set out such a selection of
models in *The New Testament World: Insights from Cultural Anthropology.* Intended as a college text, the book is highly readable and
packed with amusing and apt contemporary examples to illustrate
its principles. Let us together briefly examine the categories of first
century consciousness as he presents them, under the image of
eavesdropping on a group of foreigners, the people of the New
Testament.

Honor and Shame

After a methodological introduction, chapter 2 is devoted to
honor and shame, what Malina calls the "pivotal values" of the
New Testament world. Honor comprises two essential and complementary elements: the claim of worth and recognition of that
worth by significant others. "Ascribed honor" is that prestige and
status which comes with birth, the most secure kind of honor in the
ancient world. "Acquired honor" is that esteem earned by an individual or group by deeds of heroism or benevolence. Honor is
recognition in three major areas: power, sexual status, and religion, that is, appropriate ability to control others, appropriate
male/female roles, and appropriate relationship in the fixed hierarchy of superiors and subordinates, from one's social inferiors all
the way to God at the top of the ladder.

Individual honor must be claimed and jealously guarded by

the person; collective honor is safeguarded by a head figure, the one at the top of the hierarchy in a particular subset of the social system: the father of a family, the emperor for the empire, etc. In an "agonistic" culture, every interaction outside one's circle of familiars is a contest for honor, a challenge which must be met at the risk of loss of honor. Shame, on the other side, is not so much disgrace as it is a proper sensitivity toward one's own honor, and thus is a positive symbol.

The important points to be recognized if we are really to understand how the system works are twofold. First, it is not enough to know one's worth for oneself; it must also be publicly acknowledged. This aspect has been repeatedly brought to light in the examination of other issues, for instance customs of charity and public aid. Ancient authors who write on the subject will straightforwardly say that one of the major motivations for giving to the poor is the public gratitude and recognition of generosity that results.[1] Gospel injunctions like Matthew 6:2–8, though rooted in rabbinic traditions, were truly counter-cultural, less so in a Jewish than a Greco-Roman milieu; but remember that in New Testament times, this distinction must be made with great caution. (Notice, though, that the contrasting behavior is that of Gentiles—v. 7.)

The second important point is that honor is the greatest social value, to be preferred over wealth and even life itself. Without a good reputation, life has no meaning. Here as at many points in this discussion it will be helpful to realize that the consciousness we are describing is not only of the past but of many cultures today. In 1982 the PLO in West Beirut were under seige by Israeli forces. Asked by a reporter whether he would prefer reason (surrender and survival) or death with honor, a fifteen year old Palestinian soldier replied: "There is no alternative. If we lose our identity, we lose everything. . . . I would choose honor first. . . ." His brother added: "I would never place logic before dignity."[2]

Individual and Group

Chapter 3 of Malina's book deals with another important set of alternatives, the relationship of the individual person to his or her social structures. While the modern westerner may see development of conscience as the ability to withstand outside forces and proceed instead on one's own sense of right and wrong independently of social pressure, the first century person would rather explain conscience as the coherence of one's public image with the personal self-image. It is important that one's own self-perception match the perception of significant others.

This description should be borne in mind when reading what Paul has to say about *syneidēsis,* conscience, a favorite term (see Rom 2:15; 9:1; 13:5; 1 Cor 8:7; 10:25; 2 Cor 1:12; 5:11, etc.). Here Malina appropriately brings in a point raised many years ago by Krister Stendahl in an important article on Pauline interpretation.[3] In spite of Paul's language in Romans 7:21–23, which has been enormously misunderstood to make him sound like one possessed of a modern "guilty conscience," personal guilt is really not what Paul is talking about at all. It is rather his own self-awareness before God *and* how it matches his standing in the Christian churches that concern him.

Malina suggests that few people today bother to read any first century writings outside the New Testament because they find them boring. The reason for this is that the concerns of ancient people were very different from ours. Both writers and intended readers were asking different questions than we are. Our questions tend to be psychological and individual, largely because we are inheritors of a long tradition of individualism and more recently of "pop-psychology." It is probable that the people of the ancient world did not know each other as we do, that is, psychologically, and that therefore terms like "relationship" and "intimacy" would have meant something quite different to them than to us. Whereas we function day after day with a basic assumption of the autonomy of individuals, first century Mediterranean people lived with the assumption of the necessary and natural inherence of persons in their society. As opposed to our individualism or monadism, this is what the social sciences sometimes call "dyadism," the continual need of another in order to know one's own identity.

The dyadic person is constantly aware of inter-relationship with others as a necessary component of self-awareness and self-possession. One's position in a society both horizontally (in peer relationships) and vertically (with those of superior and inferior status) is crucial to self-perception. As we shall see in chapter 3, this need for a firmly established structure of social status had a signficant influence on the development of early Christianity. While for the modern "monadic" person the problem of growth is effective movement outside oneself into satisfying relationships, the problem for the dyadic person is the opposite: how can individuation come about, how can a person assert himself or herself over against the social grouping?

In such a society moral norms are set by and for the group to which the individual belongs and conforms. Thus responsibility for morality, stability, security, and harmony rests with the whole community. It follows then that the good of the whole has priority over the good of the individual when these principles come into conflict, for it is the identity and honor of the state, community, and family that must be upheld; the honor of the individual person has meaning only insofar as he or she is a member of those groupings.

As conclusion to this chapter, Malina presents what he calls a "three-zone model" of the dyadic personality, illustrated by many examples from biblical literature. The three zones correspond roughly though not exactly to three areas of human function and behavior as we would see them. The first zone of "emotion-fused thought" includes essentially the inner process of reflection and feeling, expressed in language of the heart, perceptible only in the eyes. The second zone of "self-expressive speech" includes the areas of communication through speech and hearing, thus clustered around the functions of mouth and ears. The third zone of "purposeful action" includes execution of intention and feeling in external movement, and is thus expressed in the functions of hands and feet. Malina suggests that this model of translating human awareness into action was an implicit pattern in which people moved and expressed themselves, and that a writer who uses the language of all three zones is implying the full range of human experience and behavior. Since language about God is largely based on the analogy of human experience, the same three-zone model is often employed to speak about divine intention and action.[4]

A problem arises here in that most of the examples given by Malina are from the Hebrew scriptures and therefore a semitic rather than Greco-Roman context, so that we are again thrown back on the Jewish vs. Greek dichotomy discussed in the previous chapter. It is certainly true that a statement from Exodus or Deuteronomy represents a different cultural world from that of Matthew or Revelation because of the Hellenistic revolution that has happened in between. Yet the same three-zone model seems to be operating in both. Citation of some examples from non-biblical literature of the first century world would have been helpful to demonstrate continuity. But again let us recall all that has been said in the last chapter about the merging of Jewish and Greek culture just before the New Testament era. It seems safe to say that the differences between Jewish and Greek ways of thinking and acting are far less significant than those between the first century dyadic personality and the twentieth century monadic one.

Limited Good

Chapter 4 of Malina's book discusses another category from the social sciences that is very helpful for understanding the differences between the New Testament world and ours, this time an economic concept. The first century Mediterranean world is a fine example of a "classic peasant society: a set of villages socially bound up with pre-industrial cities." These cities are population centers which depend on their outlying areas for basic commodities of food and clothing. The dependent country areas, in return, rely on the cities as market centers for their produce and places where manufactured and imported goods are available. Manufacturing is for the most part a small local affair: a family works together at a trade, or a more prosperous manufacturer employs a limited number of people in his workshop. In either case the tradesman-owner sells directly to the customer without intermediary agents. There are exceptions, of course: the merchant of imported goods or, in the Roman period, large brick factories under imperial or aristocratic ownership. Likewise the predominant farming model is the family farm or small farming establishment with direct marketing in an accessible city,[5] though again the vast estates of aristocrats and the feeding of a large populace like that of Rome, Antioch, or Alexandria operated on a larger and less personal scale.

In this model of peasant society and pre-industrial cities, there is normally a social stratification into four categories: urban elites, urban non-elites, villagers, and a marginal class composed of beggars and slaves. The urban elite are the only ones with the income and leisure for advanced education and literary output, and hence are the bearers of a society's traditions and standards. Moreover, it is they who control religious institutions, tax structures, and legal systems and who therefore exercise an enormous amount of social power.

Because of this controlling position of the urban elite, new movements generally begin with them and work their way down the social scale. Christianity, however, begins with the villager class, and within the first generation after the death of Jesus it has worked its way effectively into the urban non-elite group, where it continues to reside until the third century. Indeed Christianity remained an essentially urban religion until the middle ages.

I think it is important here to make a distinction between intellectual and devotional or enthusiastic movements (my own terms). It can certainly be said that in ancient societies intellectual movements originate among the urban elite, so that intellectually their circles are "where it's at," and other groups below them in the social hierarchy are always somewhat out of step or old-fashioned in comparison. The same need not always be said of movements, particularly religious ones, with a more devotional content; take for example the great popularity of oriental mystery religions in the first centuries of the Christian era. The social dynamic of the movement of Christianity has often been compared to that of these intensely missionary religions which made their way across the empire, giving new meaning and hope for salvation predominantly to the urban non-elite.[6]

In this society consisting mostly of closed, inward-looking systems of village, city, and empire, the vast majority of the population see themselves as severely limited by the social structure, as indeed they are. They are limited as well by the amount of material goods available to them. In a world with neither mass production nor the expanding horizons made possible by modern technology, any acquisition, any improvement in status is at someone else's expense. To avoid being on the wrong end of that movement neces-

sitates the cultivation of social and economic stability. Therefore
alliances of all kinds are important to ensure that stability; hence
the complex system of horizontal and vertical reciprocal relationships that grew up in ancient Mediterranean society, and that was
so essential to the smooth functioning of society. Everyday life was
built upon a vast network of patron-client relationships which en-
abled the less powerful and lower in status to know from whence
came their protection, while it gave to the more powerful and
higher in status a base of loyal support and an outlet for the generosity which was essential to the social image of their honor.

Such a society based on a perception of limited goods is almost completely without motivation by work ethic, since status
based on birth precludes advancement through work. Though
there are some exceptions to this economic determinism in the
great Roman urban centers, it remains true throughout the empire
for the vast majority of people. The poor are not those without
money but those deprived of honor by being unable to maintain
their inherited status, made so less often by financial disaster than
by political or social disgrace.

Kinship and Marriage

Chapter 5 of Malina's book examines patterns and norms that
regulate human life in relationship bound up with the life cycle of
birth and death, especially as they are revealed in four areas:
selection of marriage partners; the marriage bond; immediate family; extended family.

The Mediterranean family was a cohesive unit, a producing as
well as consuming center. Its patriarchal authority ruled over an
extended system of status structures with strong emphasis on
patrilineal continuity, often with definite preference for marriage
within the patrilineal extended family. In such a family marriage is
not a romantic choice but an institution carefully planned to further the interests of the clan. Recreational groupings are by sex,
men with men and women with women, "two exclusive circles that
might touch but never overlap." To see this custom still operative,
one need only walk through a small town in any eastern Mediterranean country today in the early evening to find the men gathered

in the local cafe while women sit in family and neighborhood groups in yards and on doorsteps exchanging conversation over their needlework.

In such close family units, bonds of loyalty are intense and members wish to remain closely localized. Honor too is a family affair, the responsibility of the patriarchal head or his male representatives to enforce and if necessary avenge. The brother-sister relationship is a primary mode of perpetuating the intense and protective loyalty of family members for one another and for the common honor of the family.

Because most of the examples in this chapter are taken from the Hebrew scriptures, it is again, like chapter 2, less directly helpful for New Testament study. We will however return to some of the concepts from this chapter in chapter 6 below when considering the household codes of the later Pauline writings.

Clean and Unclean

The final chapter from Malina's *The New Testament World* we will briefly consider because of the enormous impact of the categories of clean and unclean in the ancient world. We are dealing here with a mindset that underlies much of the legal debate between Jesus and the Jewish authorities as depicted in the synoptic gospels (see Mt 23:25–26; Mk 7:1–23; Lk 7:36–50), and is a major factor in the practical application of Paul's theology of freedom from the law. Yet it is a set of categories extremely difficult for the modern westerner to understand, a mindset which we seem to encounter today practically nowhere except in orthodox Judaism which continues it as part of the living legacy of the Mosaic law.

Rules of clean and unclean have to do with harmony and purity, with what fits and does not fit according to a perceived cosmic order. They set procedures for order in society and boundaries of behavior. They are concerned with preserving these appropriate boundaries of the social body as well as the individual body. Infraction of the rules is violation of order, and is to be carefully distinguished from moral guilt. The unclean is that which does not belong: dirt, disorder, rudeness.

These rules also set off the realms of sacred and profane, the divine and the human, from one another—a separation much more acute in ancient thinking than in ours. The categories of sacred and profane are worked out in all religions in terms of time, space, and conduct. Thus some days are meant for a special purpose, be they sabbath, Sunday, or Memorial Day. Some places are reserved for special purposes, be they temple, chapel, or the Tomb of the Unknown Soldier. Some behavior is appropriate in some times and places and not in others. Modern American society suffers from an impoverishment of these instincts of holy and ordinary, even of proper and improper. Other than the minimal rituals with which we surround sexual and excretory functions (and current debates about pornography even throw these in doubt), there are very few such observances in our lives.

Malina points out that Jesus' apparent heedlessness of the purity rules of his culture (touching lepers, healing on the sabbath, etc.), when put in the context of his debates with religious authorities, was not violation of rules but the prophetic attempt to put detailed rules within the broader context of God's sovereignty over all. The first Christian generation followed his lead by adapting the notions of holy and ordinary, clean and unclean, to their changed circumstances without a temple cult, a holy people in the midst of the world.

As I noted above, in the more formal and socially-structured sense, modern western culture seems little affected by purity rules; yet they persist in less formally sanctioned and recognized ways. In a society obsessed with physical health, they are manifest in such examples as the shunning of those who are ill and dying, and in the irrational fear of AIDS and the many ways in which its victims are loaded with implications of moral guilt. The only major difference is that as a group we split off our emotional reactions of rejection from our rational analysis. In such a society as we are describing, the rejection of uncleanness is an integrated element in a communal way of life.

Conclusion

This partial summary of the treatment of "first century consciousness" from B. Malina's *The New Testament World: Insights from Cultural Anthropology* is meant to be an invitation to read the book itself, an excellently readable introduction to the world and mentality of those who lived and wrote the New Testament. Though the book is now ten years old, it remains the best general introduction to the anthropological categories that are essential to understanding the ancient Mediterranean world.[7] My regrets are only two: that so many of the modern examples are heavily collegiate since the book is valuable for a much wider audience, and that there are not more first century non-biblical sources drawn upon rather than in some cases large numbers of Hebrew scripture examples from centuries earlier. We will have occasion to draw upon these categories, especially those of honor and shame, individual and group, and marriage and family in the discussions that follow. In Part IV we will discuss some of the more recent applications of these categories to the New Testament itself.

Part II
SLAVE AND FREE: ECONOMIC AND SOCIAL STATUS

3
The Jesus Movement

In the preceding pages we have sketched the historical, cultural, and social background of Palestine in the years that were formative for the setting of Jesus' ministry. Now it is time to turn our attention to the people who were caught up in that movement. Who were they? From what backgrounds? What motivated them and what were the social patterns within the movement itself in the first years? How did Jesus and his followers relate to the economic and social structures of their world? These are some of the questions that have been asked by recent writers who have attempted to observe the Jesus movement through the lens of social science models.

Palestinian Society

Since the first followers of Jesus were all Palestinians and mostly Galileans, it will be helpful to look at the social stratification of Palestine, and especially of Galilee at the time as outlined by Freyne and those working with macrosociological analysis of social stratification, such as A.J. Saldarini, *Pharisees, Scribes and Sadducees: A Sociological Approach.*[1] According to the conclusions of this analysis, based largely on Gerhard Lenski,[2] the first century Mediterranean world falls in the category of a pre-industrial advanced agrarian society. In such a society, the economic base is agricultural production in a complex hierarchical system that serves the needs of a small urban elite.

At the base of the economic and social system were the peasants (Malina's "villagers"), who constituted by far the majority of
the population, probably more than seventy percent. Theirs was an
ancestral and largely unchanging rural way of life, whether as owners of their own land or as tenant farmers. Some of their population were forcibly changed from landowners to tenants or other
kinds of subsistence laborers by temporary agricultural disasters
from which they never recovered their independence. They were
largely uninvolved in the wider commercial activity and thus less
influenced by Hellenism than other groups. Their focus was village
life with its closed patterns of kinship and loyalty that remained
relatively unchanged while empires came and went. They would be
the sector of the population most conscious of the problem of
"limited good," for theirs was subsistence existence, whose primary concern was not what surplus would be left over, but
whether, after those above them claimed what they had the power
to take, there would be enough on which to live.

Associated with the peasant farmers were the "rural proletariat"—the rootless day laborers, itinerant craftsmen, and brigands of
the countryside and villages. These were people with their origins
and sympathies with the peasant class, but with less stability and
more unrest in their lives brought on by greater economic and social
pressures (consider the day laborers of Matthew 20:1–16 who are at
the mercy of the vinegrower's whim). Because of their subsistence
living without access to the land with all its symbolic as well as
economic significance, they had less to lose than the land-bound
peasants by looking for alternatives to their present existence.

The local artisans of this group, perhaps three to seven percent of the population, supported the needs of the peasant class for
products of wood, metal, and stone. They supplied basic agricultural and household items. Some were peasant farmers forced off
the land. Those fortunate enough to have skills and materials mar-
ketable to elite urban consumers may have fared well, but most of
their customers were at the poverty level. It is among these village
artisans that the gospels place Jesus of Nazareth.

Just above the peasant class in the Roman period was a merchant class composed of some free persons but also largely of the
slaves and freedmen/women of the elite who carried on most of the

commerce that was not directly connected to taxation. They were closely bound into a patron-client relationship with elites and, like all other non-elites, had little social mobility. Yet they may have had more than most, just because of the small amount of capital available to them. However, they were just as much part of the pyramidal economic system as any others.

Another level of society was made up by what Lenski calls "retainers," a class of bureaucrats, civil servants, military and religious professionals whose function was to support the economic and social system by serving the needs of the elite as extensions of their power. This group developed in Palestine in the earlier Persian and Hellenistic systems, probably originally consisting of members of the foreign occupying nationality. By the time of Jesus, however, they were nearly all Jewish: local judges and civil administrators, lesser tax collectors, stewards of absentee landlords, most with no great love for their social inferiors (compare the hostility of tenants for stewards and landlords in Mark 12:2–8 with the steward's manipulation of tenants in Luke 16:1–8).

Tax collectors were especially despised by their inferiors because they were collaborators with foreign occupiers who preyed on their own people for their own advantage. Though the scribes may not have been an identifiable social group, being rather a profession that endured through many changes of culture and government, inasmuch as they could be located as a class, they probably belonged here. Likewise, the Pharisees have been elusive and notoriously difficult to locate by class, since they were a religious interest group whose occupations in the first century are uncertain. They too may have belonged to this class (Saldarini).

At the top of the pyramid in Palestinian society were the urban elites who constituted a very small proportion of the population, probably no more than three percent. They owed their status to the Hellenistic urbanization of Palestine and to Herod the Great's distribution of land to his supporters some fifty years before. Their continued status depended on their continuing ability to placate Herodian and Roman interests. Residents of Jerusalem or of Tiberias or Sepphoris in Galilee, they often owned vast estates confiscated from peasants who had fallen victim to taxation, and tax concessions whose control depended on the pleasure of ruling authorities. Their income derived principally from taxation of the land, and thus the economic burden of their support fell ultimately through bureaucratic levels onto the peasants.

The "Herodians" of the gospels may have belonged to this group (Mk 3:6; 12:13). Part of this elite class consisted of the priestly families whose control of the temple kept them at the top of the flow of wealth and close to sources of political power. The Sadducees formed part, but not the whole, of this priestly elite, for whom the smooth running of the religious establishment meant not only their livelihood but the maintenance of their status, dependent on the will of Roman authority.

The picture of Palestinian society that emerges is of a steep and tightly structured pyramid in which the needs of a small elite minority are met by the exploited labor of the majority by means of an intermediate class whose status and livelihood depend on serving the few and exploiting the many. Tempting as it may be, we must avoid identifying this intermediate group as a "middle class," a term that in a modern industrialized society connotes something entirely different. This intermediate class in ancient Palestinian society neither was a majority nor had any real economic or social mobility.

When trying to establish clearly defined social classes in any society, we must remember that the actual situation was more complex than anything that can be neatly classified, and that from such a distance in time it is extremely difficult to construct societal patterns which were much more a matter of everyday unspoken experience than literary record. Nevertheless, some general lines do emerge, and these can be spoken of as we do here. An important thing to remember is that in the Mediterranean world status depended far less on income and lifestyle than on birth and inherited situation. In contemporary American society social class is an illusive reality with fluid boundaries that are easily crossed by changes in income, job status, education, and change of location. Whatever the reality, the democratic ideal holds that all are citizens with identical rights and that the possibility of social and economic betterment is open to all. Though we shall later see that there were some exceptions, generally Greco-Roman society was quite different. Privilege, wealth, and full civil rights belonged only to those born into a certain status, who passed it on to the next generation. Those without it could give their progeny only more of the inferior status that had been theirs for generations.

Early Christianity as Millenarianism

With these social factors as backdrop, many have tried to understand just what was the appeal of Jesus' preaching to those who first followed him and how his quick popularity is explainable in terms of what we know of the life of those first followers. One of the first writers of the new social science approach to tackle these questions was John Gager in *Kingdom and Community: The Social World of Early Christianity.* Drawing upon the research of cultural anthropologists regarding other known millenarian movements,[3] Gager attempts in his second chapter to understand the dynamics of Jesus' ministry and the early years of the church as a movement of dramatic expectation.

The term "millenarianism" as used here bears no necessary relation to the idea of Christ's thousand-year reign on earth as narrated in Revelation 20:1–7. Rather it refers to the expectation of "a new order of reality in the near future,"[4] a reversal of the present order in which wrongs will be righted. Such movements are usually characterized by a quick burst of enthusiasm and short life span, often centered around a charismatic, prophetic leader who is not necessarily the cause of the movement but serves to focus its energy and embody its new vision in himself/herself.

Because of the belief in the imminent reversal of the social order, the group usually begins to live out this vision in initial ways: social and/or sexual egalitarianism and the minimizing of social structures. There is a strong sense of boundaries, of who belongs and who doesn't, and these norms of membership and status tend to reverse those of the larger society, over against which the millenarian group sees itself: those who think themselves in the "in" group are really "out of it," and vice versa (see Mk 10:31; Mt 20:16; Lk 13:30: "The first shall be last and the last first," the same saying in three entirely different contexts).

To whom would such a movement most appeal? Much but not all research indicates of course the disinherited, the disadvantaged of society, who have the most to gain by having the tables turned. Characteristically, money and its related activities are seen as sources of corruption and perverted symbols of human worth, whereas the new order will provide heavenly compensation for poverty and restore the proper criteria for human dignity (see Mt 5:3; Lk 6:20–26; Mk 10:21–23; Jas 2:5; 5:1–6). If the appeal is not always to those at the very bottom of the social scale, it is at least to those who experience "relative deprivation," the frustration of unfulfilled hopes and the insecurity of an uncertain future. The hopelessness of the unenlightened oppressed may actually constitute a society that is harder to shake loose, whereas those who are aware of their plight and have had their hopes stirred up are a dangerously volatile force.

As must be obvious by now, the model of millenarian groups is a helpful perspective from which to approach the first years of the Jesus movement. Other apocalyptic preachers are known to have surfaced in Palestine in the years prior to Jesus' ministry, and many of the later books of the Hebrew scriptures (Ezekiel, Daniel, Second and Third Isaiah, etc.) hold out the promise of just such a reversal of the social order, where peace and prosperity will be open to all under the reign of God. Jesus' insistence on the transcendent element of the kingdom which is nevertheless here and now (Mk 1:14; Mt 12:28; 19:14; Lk 13:28–29) did not prevent even his closest disciples from thinking that a political revolution was in the offing (Acts 1:6). The strong call to justice, integrity, and peace would have appealed most strongly precisely to those most conscious that they were being deprived of it: the peasants and village craftspersons (the group from which Jesus himself came), the marginalized and the dispossessed.

In saying this, however, we must beware of being overly simplistic or romantic. Many such people were not at all poverty-stricken: Zebedee had hired laborers (Mk 1:20) and skilled artisans held a certain status in village society. Moreover, one of the disciples was a tax collector, and Jesus attracted the favorable attention of a synagogue official (Mk 5:22), a Pharisee (Lk 7:36), a rich member of a town council (Mt 27:57; Lk 23:50–51), even a Roman military officer (Lk 7:2–10). One of the remarkable characteristics of Jesus' ministry is his ability to move in and out of various status groups: peasants, townspeople, tax collectors and prostitutes (who, though they are lumped together in Matthew 21:31–32, would by no means have identified with each other), Pharisees and well-to-do urbanites. The key to social class in the Mediterranean world was not income but *status*. Usually but not always, wealth or lack of it was proportionate to status.

With that qualification raised, still it can be said that there are great similarities between what we know of the origins of the Jesus movement and other millenarian movements. Those people in the most vulnerable positions in society were the most ready to hear the apocalyptic message of hope that the evil ways of the present system could soon be reversed in a gigantic sweeping action of God's just hand.

Cognitive Dissonance

It has long been a question among scholars of early Christianity how the expectation of an imminent and cataclysmic end of the present order was transformed into an historical faith. Whatever was Jesus' intention, it can hardly be doubted that the oral tradition about him and the New Testament writings contain definite elements of such an expectation (see for instance Mk 9:1; 13:30; 1 Thes 4:15–17). What happened when the parousia, the final coming of Christ, was delayed? The apocalyptic message had to be reinterpreted and accommodated to a way of life intended to continue indefinitely in history: imminent expectation became continual watchfulness, the apocalyptic symbols became ways of interpreting history.

In the second section of chapter 2 of *Kingdom and Community,* Gager draws on another social science theory to interpret the early Christian response to the delay of the parousia: cognitive dissonance.[5] This theory, based on the study of many apocalyptic-prophetic groups, postulates that when a group's fundamental religious beliefs are disconfirmed, one possible result is dissolution, but this is not the only possibility. Instead, the group may intensify its fervor and translate this energy into an expanded missionary movement. The greater the dissonance between expectation and result, the greater the need to reassess, reinterpret, and convert others.

Thus the disciples' expectation that Jesus during his life would establish the earthly kingdom of God was disconfirmed in the totally disconcerting event of his crucifixion. Even though the gospels portray Jesus as having predicted it during his lifetime (Mk 8:31–33; 9:31–32; 10:33–34, with parallels in Matthew and Luke), the consistent reaction of the disciples is disbelief and lack of comprehension, even after they have heard reports of his having been raised (Lk 24:21–24). Indeed they seem to have been, understandably, more bewildered by this than by his death. Soon they came to the realization that the resurrection was partly confirming of their expectations, yet it intensified expectation of the final coming, for which it was seen as an imminent preparation.

The delay of the parousia became a second element of disconfirmation, however. This is reflected as a problem in such texts as 2 Peter 3:3–10 and James 5:7–9 with their message of patient hope for the coming of the Lord who is nevertheless on the way despite an apparent slowdown in the projected time frame. Again, disconfirmation seems to evoke a renewal of fervor, a reassessment and recommitment to a firm belief and way of life and vigorous attempts to convert others. The support of group reinforcement is crucial for continued survival and vitality of belief; of this element there is no lack of evidence in the strong community structure of early Christianity as we see it manifested especially in Acts and the Pauline epistles.

The confusion caused by disconfirmation of the expectation brings two different kinds of response in a group that survives the crisis: the intellectual response of reassessment and reinterpretation (we misunderstood; the timing was wrong; patient waiting is more important than realization), and the social response of proselytism or mission activity (the compulsion to carry forth the word and expand the number of believers). Both elements can clearly be seen operating in the first years of Christianity, and Gager has alerted us to an important new perspective from which to examine the New Testament events.

The weakest point in the application of cognitive dissonance theory to early Christianity is in my opinion the function of the resurrection which, as much as it seems to have taken the disciples by surprise, can only be seen within the scope of the theory as a strongly *confirming* faith event which generated energy to eclipse almost totally the disconfirmation of Jesus' death among believers and the delay of his final coming as well, enabling the reinterpretation of the parousia to be made with more ease. Admittedly the "scandal of the cross" in missionary efforts among belivers remained a serious obstacle (1 Cor 1:20–25). But cognitive dissonance theory and Gager's analysis are concerned primarily with the inner dynamics of the group of believers.

The final section of chapter 2 of *Kingdom and Community* deals with the book of Revelation as exemplar of the way in which apocalyptic vision can be a means of sublimated attainment of millennial bliss through a sort of therapeutic purification. Though the social function of apocalyptic literature is an object of much current interest, the treatment in this section is done within a more psychoanalytic framework, which takes us outside the scope of the present investigation. Those interested in the psychic structure of symbolic function will find it helpful.

Wandering Charismatics

Another recent writer who has attempted to apply social science models to what we know of the early Jesus movement is Gerd Theissen, whose work first appeared in German in 1977 as a "sociology of the Jesus movement," with English translation the next year entitled more generally *Sociology of Early Palestinian Christianity.*[6] His procedure is to investigate roles, other social factors, and functions of early Christianity in its original environment under three aspects: constructive conclusions assembling data, analytic conclusions regarding function, and comparative conclusions relating these factors to other possibly related situations in the Greco-Roman world.

Examining the evidence of the gospels, Theissen proposes that Jesus did not establish communities, but groups of itinerants with a lifestyle characterized by renunciation of home, family, possessions, and protection, a lifestyle quite similar to that of itinerant Cynic philosophers in the Greek world and possibly influenced by it. These "wandering charismatics" were the core of Jesus' followers, materially supported wherever they went by "local sympathizers" grouped in communities. These resident sympathizers were less radical in their lifestyle than the itinerants, and their ethos depended largely on the principles of behavior and procedure enunciated in the gospels.

The focus of both groups was of course Jesus himself, the "bearer of revelation," whose proclamation of the imminent kingdom gave meaning to the counter-societal aspects of this Jewish reform movement. As Son of Man suffering (Mk 8:31; 9:31; 10:33–34) and soon to be glorified (Mk 8:38; 13:26; Mt 19:28), his identity and destiny bore enormously on their own, for their fate was the same: his suffering is mirrored in theirs, his glorification is the promise of theirs. Christology explains life.

Theissen goes on to examine the socio-economic, political, and cultural situation with the method given above, concluding that the "social rootlessness" which Jesus' wandering disciples exemplified (but which was not limited to them) was related to socio-economic factors of ambiguity and survival situations for some peasants and villagers in Palestine at this time. The tensions between rural and urban, upper and lower classes, wealthy and poor, foreign and indigenous, were deepening. Those with least to lose by abandoning social roots were the already dispossessed or squeezed out, of whatever class: peasants, a "marginal middle class" caught in-between, those who have known a better and more honorable way of living and have lost it. It is they who are most sensitive to suffering and deprivation, who yearn for deliverance of one kind or another, whereas those comfortably secure in whatever position are less acquainted with their own need for redemption. Jesus was a rural leader who avoided the great urban centers except the unavoidable Jerusalem.

The observant reader will note that much of the preceding paragraph sounds familiar. Theissen's socio-economic analyses in this book and other writings were a partial influence on Freyne's *Galilee*. Freyne has more carefully documented the literary, historical, archaeological, and inscriptional evidence, tried some of Theissen's analyses, and found them to fit.

In regard to the political significance of the Jesus movement,

Theissen characterizes it as a reform intended to purify and radicalize an already theoretically existing theocracy. The political crisis of the era for Judaism was the possibility of reviving the theocratic vision after a recent parade of foreign and less than successful native rulers. The Jesus movement differed from most of the radical theocratic reform movements because, rather than incorporate anti-foreign sentiment as an essential ingredient, it preached a sometimes cautious yet persistent universalism—a factor which was ultimately to contribute to its downfall in Palestine and success in the diaspora.

It is a sociological principle that one reaction to crisis is an intensification of norms, a renewal movement which will call members to a deepened commitment to the group and its original qualities. In the face of invasion by Hellenistic culture, most Jewish reform movements stressed more intense dedication to traditional cultural and religious values: the law (Pharisees), the temple (Sadducees), exclusivist notions of priesthood (Essenes). While some traditions about Jesus' preaching stressed respect for these traditions (e.g. Mt 5:17–19), others challenged them with universalist claims that transcended Jewish ethnocentrism (e.g. Mk 7:14–19; Mt 28:19–20), picked up the universalist trends of post-exilic prophecy, and laid the foundations for a missionary movement that could thrive in the cosmopolitan pluralistic environment of the Roman world.

Challenge to Functionalism

Theissen has been criticized for an absence of explicit sociological theory underlying his social assumptions. Like Gager, he also dips occasionally into psychoanalytic models, a far more questionable procedure given the dearth of individualized data and the vast differences in consciousness as described in Malina's *New Testament World* discussed in chapter 2 above. Theissen also has a tendency to maintain too sharply the distinction between "Palestinian" and "Hellenistic" Judaism, despite his knowledge and use of Hengel's work.

The sharpest critique of Theissen has been leveled by R.A. Horsley in *Sociology and the Jesus Movement*. He takes issue with

Theissen for his implicit reliance on the sociological model of structural functionalism, which might be described as the theory that all aspects of society relate to each other in an integral way that contributes to the stabilization of that society; social change is the adjustment of a society to a new element in order to integrate it into the organic whole. To put it negatively, according to the accusation of its critics, the theory reinforces the status quo of present structures and allows for no essential role for creative conflict. Thus, charges Horsley, it is most appealing to American and northern European biblical scholars who consider themselves critical and objective exegetes and historians, but whose interests in fact align them with the forces of political stabilization and resistance to change. As a member of this social group, Theissen has created a Jesus movement that serves the interests of social stabilization rather than social change, and in which there is no room for structural conflict. He perceptively asks: If the Jesus movement did indeed contribute to social stabilization rather than change, why were people like Jesus and Paul executed? There is more to the story.

Horsley then goes on to construct an alternative model of the Jesus movement based not on functionalism but on another sociological model, conflict theory, which posits that society is made up of conflicting and competing forces, and that social change happens not as adjustment and stabilization after the introduction of a new element as in functionalism, but as clash of contradictory forces fighting for control. Thus the Jesus movement would have begun as a kind of peasant revolt against the oppressive ruling establishment, not military in nature, but a resistance to the continuation of the status quo.

Horsley agrees with Theissen that the Jesus movement was a social renewal movement, but of entire local communities, not just of the wandering charismatics. Conflicts present in the gospels represent not only religious or ideological, but social and economic clashes between peasants and "retainers" in the person of scribes, Pharisees, and Sadducees, representing the interests of central power.

Sociology and the Jesus Movement represents the most thorough critique of Theissen's work, and one of the best attempts to construct an alternative based on a different model of social dynamics. Horsley acknowledges that the extent of his critique is itself a tribute to the foundational importance of Theissen's study. Yet Horsley also yields to the temptation to fill in the gaps with conjecture where evidence or even theory backed up with data is lacking.

There can be no doubt that Horsley's reconstruction of a peasant renewal movement as voice of the oppressed in a society in upheaval contains important elements neglected by Theissen's portrayal. Certainly it is more appealing to readers who espouse the conflict model or find themselves in advocacy positions in an oppressive system. The attempt to portray accurately the significance of Jesus and his first followers in their own context will continue.

4
Paul and the People of His World

Some years ago a TV special[1] followed the missionary careers of Peter and Paul as they moved out of the Palestinian context into the larger world of the Roman empire in its finest years. After a good many years of more or less successful evangelizing in the quieter towns of Asia Minor, Cyprus, and Macedonia, Paul began to set his sights on the intellectual center of Athens. He was warned by friends that the sophisticated citizens of the "big city" would not be as receptive to his philosophically unpalatable message as had been the less sophisticated people with whom he had been dealing in more backward areas.

The enthusiastic Paul ignored the warning, marched into Athens, and proceeded to address the intellectual types gathered on the Areopagus—somewhat equivalent to giving a public lecture in a university town—with the speech attributed to him in Acts 17. Sure enough, the warning came true. In spite of the clever beginning in which he claimed to know the unknown god whom they worshiped without knowing, at the mention of the resurrection of Jesus he was met by laughter and mockery. The notion of bodily resurrection was rejected as naive wishful thinking from some backwater place like Palestine.

Though any modern depiction of New Testament events includes some exaggeration for the sake of effect, there is an element of truth in the way the story is told. Paul was a man of the Greco-Roman world, a native Greek speaker, a Hellenistic Jew. His Greek background was of inestimable value to him in his work in the diaspora mission. Yet his rabbinic education brought him into direct contact with the literary and theological sources of his faith and ethnic culture. As a Pharisee he represented one of the most prominent and progressive groups in the Palestinian Judaism of his day. Paul's challenge was to translate faith in Jesus from a rural peasant language to that of a sophisticated urban culture. In the process, like any creative and visionary thinker, he made many friends and many enemies.

The Cosmopolitan World of the Christian Mission

The Roman world of Paul's day was a civilization that had never been surpassed for the grandeur of its undertakings. The artistic and intellectual inheritance of Greece, from which the Romans never begged but freely borrowed and stole, was combined with Roman superiority in technology and political organization to produce a way of life that unified the Mediterranean world from one end to the other in a common urban civilization.

Like any civilization, it had its systems of social stratification whose subtleties are somewhat elusive to us who are separated from it by time and distance. Nevertheless a great deal can be known about the social system of the Roman imperial period, the time of the writing of the New Testament. It was a system that worked horizontally and vertically in different ways from a modern western culture, where social status depends mostly on economic level and affordable lifestyle, where the nuclear family is the norm, and where the democratic ideal precludes formal stratification of society into a hierarchy of superiors and inferiors.

The ancient world, on the other hand, did not associate economic level and social status as closely as we do. Rather, the status into which one was born was usually accompanied by a corresponding economic level, but with rare exceptions it was the family and legal status to which one belonged that mattered far more than financial affluence or lack of it. The hierarchical extended family concept at every level of society created a coherent pattern of social structure with clear positions of superiority and subordination (this will be further developed in chapter 6 when we examine the intent of the household codes in the later books of the New Testament).

The Roman social order[2] was topped by two very small groups or *ordines* of aristocrats—first, the senatorial *ordo* whose members were eligible for the highest civil and religious posts; second, the lesser aristocratic *ordo* of the equestrians or knights who formed the backbone of second-rung administrators in the empire. Pontius Pilate, Felix and Festus (Acts 23—25), successive prefects of Judea, were probably equestrians, answerable to a senatorial-rank governor in Syria like the earlier Quirinius (see Lk 2:2). As these two aristocratic *ordines* became decimated by civil wars and political purges, their ranks were filled by members of the aristocratic families from the occupied provinces, who naturally brought with them not only their ethnic and cultural differences, but diverse worldviews as well. The aristocratic Roman sentiments of nobility, virtue, and conservatism idealized by the old senatorial families slowly gave way to the sophisticated cosmopolitan outlook of the newer set out to make their own way in the world and serve Rome at the same time.

Below the ranks of aristocrats were the freeborn urban lower classes, about whom we know least of all, perhaps because their lot changed the least from generation to generation. The quiet backbone of the free labor force, they went about their lives without leaving much of an effect on either the literary or archaeological evidence that has survived. In Rome at least there were regular distributions of free grain for them out of the imperial treasury, and in all major urban centers public banquets, celebrations, and entertainment were provided chiefly with them in mind by both public and private beneficence.

In the urban social structure as described here, an important and ambiguous role is played by slaves and freedmen/women. Whether born into slavery or enslaved as abandoned foundlings, war captives, victims of debt or kidnaping, or convicted criminals, slaves had no legal rights and were theoretically non-persons. On agricultural estates (slave agriculture was practiced mostly in Italy), in galley ships and in mines theirs was an unenviable lot. Even in the urban context they could be put to the hard and degrading kinds of labor that free persons were thus spared.

Urban slavery had other and less degrading aspects, however. Household slaves often had a great deal of independence and responsibility. Teachers and financial managers were often slaves. Much of the effective administration of the imperial civil service with its vast international network was in the hands of the imperial slaves and freedmen. Statistical studies of the inscriptional and literary evidence of the period show that a high number of slaves received their freedom ("manumission") in midlife, males often to become trusted superintendents of their previous owner's goods, females often to become their previous owner's legal wife.

Legally and theoretically, slaves had no status whatsoever. Yet in a typical example of the ability of Mediterranean cultures to tolerate ambiguity, a series of laws and customs developed over the years protecting slaves from the cruelty of owners. And, in fact, slaves were socially embedded in the household and status of their owners, so that they shared derivatively in that status.

Many freedmen/women became successful in business or civil service, advanced socially as well as economically, and became rich and powerful. It was not unusual for a family over the span of two or three generations to go from slavery to a fairly well-to-do economic and social level, and eventually perhaps even to gain access to the equestrian *ordo* and beyond. The second century freedman philosopher Epictetus lamented that slaves dream only about emancipation, then making money, entering the equestrian *ordo*, gaining a military command and eventually access to the senate, where they would find themselves more enslaved by their situation than when they were actually slaves.[3] The comment is to be taken as social commentary as well as philosophical satire.

If the freedmen/women class had the least to lose, they had the most to gain. As *nouveaux riches* they could be ostentatious and overbearing with their wealth. The literature of the period is punctuated with the resentful comments of aristocrats who consider their displays of pomp tasteless. This is not to assume that every emancipated slave became wealthy, but a good number apparently did, enough to give the whole group the reputation for being socially and commercially aggressive. The goal for which they yearned was the cultured and leisured life of the landed aristocracy.

No matter how hard they worked or how wealthy they became

however, freedmen were still bound for life to a client relationship with their former owner as patron, and still excluded from full acceptance into that ruling group and from the most prestigious political appointments and positions (though their descendants might gain access to them). This difference, made officially by social stratification and reinforced unofficially by discrimination, marks the distinction between *ordo* as juridically and hierarchically understood, and social class as a more fluid indicator of one's power based on wealth and influence. Both factors operated in the New Testament world as conditions affecting what one could or could not do. Paul's famous comment in 1 Corinthians 1:27 probably refers to both systems: not many of the Corinthian Christians, he says, were sophisticated or powerful (probably indicators of education, culture, wealth, and influence) or well-born (definitely an indicator of hierarchical social status by family). The examples of women are also illustrative: though women are known throughout Roman times to have participated in business and trade guilds and to have exercised considerable influence through wealth and social position, no woman is ever known to have held a major political or administrative appointment (precisely those positions reserved for the hierarchically elite group), and the structural position of women in Roman society always remained inferior to that of men.

There are of course many other characteristics of the Roman urban world which affected the New Testament. Several more can be briefly singled out as significant: the patron-client relationship, various types of social organizations, and the function of mobility.[4]

Because of the different types of social stratification described above, people in the Roman world did not generally assume that "all are created equal," or at least that equality was given in social relations. Rather, the ranking of some as superior and others as inferior on the basis of birth, family, or position led to an elaborate structuring of relationships between social unequals on the basis of a patronage system that greatly enhanced the smooth operation of society. The beneficent and generous protection of the great was expected in return for the gratitude, adulation, and faithful service of the dependent. Thus one of the best ways to gain social advancement and preference was to ingratiate oneself with a powerful person from whose generosity one hoped to benefit. The system extended from the private to the public level. Even kings owed their position to those more powerful, as clients of their patron: the relation of the Herodian rulers in Palestine to the Roman emperor is a good example. Public works for the benefit of citizens were often financed by wealthy patrons, thus placing a whole populace in the position of client. In such a society, intricate patterns of dependence develop and overlap, creating a fabric of loyalties that is an important part of the social structure.

If the patron-client system fostered unequal relationships, the system of social clubs or organizations encouraged the interchange of equals. Some were predominantly religious organizations, formed around the cult of a certain deity, others were formed on the basis of a common trade or occupation, still others were burial societies, whose principal purpose seems to have been the collection of funds to ensure a suitable and dignified burial of the members. Such organizations, usually called *collegia* in Latin or *thiasoi* in Greek, were not unidimensional, however, for the characteristics of all three of these types could be, and frequently were, combined in one grouping. The club may sometimes have been sustained by a wealthy patron or patroness, but members could be freeborn or freed, even slaves in some cases, usually male but also on occasion female. The associations had membership dues, entrance fees, a constitution, and officers with important-sounding titles. Though often organized on the basis of common occupations, they did not function like medieval trade guilds or modern labor unions but seem to have been mostly social in nature.

It was suggested long ago that this kind of organization may have been the basic model for the urban Christian communities, for whom common cult was certainly the major element, and whom we know at least from the end of the second century to have taken it upon themselves to provide for the burial of members. It is now generally accepted that whatever the similarities between the two types of groups, there are sufficient dissimilarities that Christian communities would probably not have been seen as just another kind of *thiasos* among many.

Because of the excellent road system that was one of the benefits of Roman rule, the possibilities for mobility on the part of

even non-royalty and non-military in the Roman world were unri-
valed. The first century of the Christian era was a time of enormous commercial prosperity and exchange, when major trade centers like Antioch, Thessalonica, Corinth, and Rome saw people
from the ends of the Mediterranean world pass through them ply-
ing their trades. The great urban centers were the places in which
not only commerce but literary and intellectual discourse took
place, fed by the steady stream of travelers who passed through
and often stayed a while, philosophers and scholars as well as
traders and business people. Because of this high degree of travel
and mobility, new ideas as well as foreign goods could reach everywhere. The Christians in Paul's world who seem to be frequently
on the move (besides Paul himself and his missionary companions), e.g. Prisca and Aquila (Acts 18:2, 18, etc.), Lydia the cloth
merchant at Philippi (Acts 16:14), Phoebe of Cenchrae bound for
Rome (Rom 16:1–2), and Apollos of Alexandria (Acts 18:24; 1
Cor 1:12), to name only a few, are probably not exceptions to a
common pattern. They may in fact have taken advantage of business trips to do religious work as well—or vice versa.

Paul's Social Status

Having seen some of the factors which created the social and
cultural environment in which Pauline Christianity flourished, let
us now turn to Paul himself and attempt to situate him in that
environment.

We know a number of things about Paul relevant to his social
status. From Paul's own letters we know that he was a Jew and
belonged to that religious party within Judaism known as the Pharisees. From his writing style we know that his Greek literary education was adequate, and that he was also well versed in the methods
of biblical exegesis that he could only have learned by study with
Jewish scholars. We know from 1 Corinthians 9 and elsewhere that
on principle he refused to accept financial support from most of the
communities he served, but insisted on earning his own sustenance
by working at a manual skill even though the opposite was customary for apostles. An exception seems to have been Philippi in

Macedonia, from whose Christians he accepted gifts (see Phil 4:14–18; 2 Cor 11:8–9).

From the Acts of the Apostles we learn other details about Paul's social standing which Paul himself does not mention, chiefly that he was a citizen of the city of Tarsus in southeastern Asia Minor and a Roman citizen as well. In addition, it is Acts which specifies that his trade was tentmaking, which probably means leather working in general. Because the author seems to have definite literary and theological purposes in the presentation of some material, the data from Acts must be used with caution. But, on the other hand, they are not to be ignored.

Ronald Hock, in *The Social Context of Paul's Ministry,* attempts to situate Paul in his social milieu by means of his trade. He points out first of all that the term given by Acts for Paul's trade, *skēnopoios,* can refer to any kind of working with tanned leather— stitching tents, making shoes, leather binding, etc. Paul gives evidence of having had a literary education that would have placed him in a different social grouping than that of leather craftsmen.[5] What is he doing in the workshop?

The traditional way of understanding this mixture of roles has been to attribute it to Paul's Jewish sub-culture and especially to his rabbinic training. Later rabbinic advice praises the combination of study of the law with some other occupation. Hock questions this association, and suggests that instead we look to the wider Greco-Roman culture in which Paul participated. There we find the model of the Stoic-Cynic philosopher, the best known type of sage figure in his day. The philosophers were able to support themselves in one or more of four ways: charging fees for their instruction, attaching themselves as clients to wealthy patrons as "scholar in residence" in the household, begging (the most extreme alternative which only the hardiest chose), or working at some form of trade by which they could be self-employed, earning only as much as they needed for their bodily needs while still having time to devote to teaching and study. Some who chose this last alternative even carried on philosophical discourse in the setting of the workshop, a tradition that goes back at least as far as Socrates.

To understand this association with Paul, we must recall that a "philosophy" in the Hellenistic world is not merely an intellectual system debated by scholars. It is rather a way of living wisely which is proposed by its teachers to whoever can grasp it in order to know the way of truth and live accordingly. Sometimes followers of a particular philosopher lived together in a communal ascetic lifestyle. With this in mind, one can see how early Christian communities were often seen as "philosophies" and hence its teachers as "philosophers."

In a previous article[6] Hock had developed the argument that not only what we know of Paul's education, but even his terminology and attitudes toward work classify him as one from "the socially privileged classes" who has voluntarily taken on a trade which otherwise would be socially beneath him. Here Hock goes on to argue that the principal reason for Paul's insistence on earning his own way is his wish to identify with the most dignified way of life of the philosopher, with one who is neither mercenary in charging fees nor servile in being dependent on a wealthy patron. Paul's insistence on his freedom in 1 Corinthians 9:1,19 would echo this sentiment.

Apparently the Corinthian Christians were not pleased by this stand on Paul's part (see 1 Cor 9; 2 Cor 11:7–11; 12:13–16). This may have been because they thought such manual labor was demeaning for their apostle, whereas the "super apostles" against whom Paul contends in 2 Corinthians 11 and 12 either followed the usual custom of accepting hospitality from the communities, or had more dignified means of livelihood. Another reason, of course, may have been that Paul was thus more independent and less answerable to them. Still a third possible reason, suggested by G. Theissen (whose book on Pauline Christianity will be discussed below), is that the "command of the Lord" cited by Paul in 1 Corinthians 9:14 about missionaries getting their living from the gospel was intended not so much to compel communities authoritatively to support their missionaries as it was to compel missionaries to live in voluntary poverty, dependent upon the generosity of others. According to this explanation, Paul balks at taking this radical stand for his own reasons, and the Corinthians are attempting to recall him to his responsibility as they see it.

Whatever the reason for Paul's insistence on economic independence from most of his communities, his position echoes the ideal of simplicity and independence proposed particularly by the Stoic philosophers, but also represented in the Jewish wisdom tradition. This notion of *autarkeia,* or "self-sufficiency," later became a strong theme in Christian monasticism. It represents a middle ground between radical asceticism on the one hand and enslavement to one's passions and desires on the other. By being independent of human means and therefore of social pressures, as well as remaining indifferent to the needs and wants of the appetites, the person who is *autarkēs* could be truly free, inwardly and outwardly. Paul's strongest expressions of this ideal for himself are his warning against enslavement to passion in 1 Corinthians 6:12 and his remarks about being content whether in abundance or want in Philippians 4:11–13.[7] Such attitudes are most likely to come from one who has had the education, leisure, and prosperity to know both sides of the situation and critically reflect on his experience.

Class, Status, and Conflict at Corinth

Having seen what we can surmise about Paul's social status, let us now turn to the investigation of the status of the first generation of Christians in the cities of the Roman world. At the beginning of this century came discoveries of many written documents from the ordinary life of people in the same era as that of the New Testament. These thousands of legal contracts, personal letters, dinner invitations, elementary school exercises, etc. were preserved on papyrus in the hot dry climate of Egypt. These discoveries revolutionized the study of biblical Greek by making scholars aware that the language of the New Testament was much closer to the ordinary spoken Greek of the day than they had thought. The documents seemed to confirm the accusation of the second century pagan philosopher Celsus that Christians came from and addressed themselves to only the lowest classes in society, the ignorant, the poor, the credulous. The language of these everyday documents suggested to the great scholar of papyrology, G.A. Deissmann, that the New Testament was written by and for members of the middle and lower classes, since much of it reflected the same style,

devoid of the better classicist literary style known from the more
sophisticated literature of the same period.[8]

Since Deissmann, however, others have questioned these conclusions, notably the Australian classicist, E.A. Judge, who suggested in a little book published in 1960 that the evidence both of
the New Testament itself and of social patterns in its environment
indicates much more of a social mix, and particularly the influence
of persons of higher social status and prosperity who would have
been looked to for leadership and financial support after the pattern of the patron-client relationship.[9] Since then there has been
somewhat of a growing consensus that Christianity as it moved into
the urban society of the Roman world was not so much a popular
movement of the poor and dispossessed (the "proletariat" of earlier Marxist interpreters) as it was a truly cross-sectional representation of Greco-Roman society, with the possible omission of the
highest *ordines* and the lowest "dregs."

Recently there have appeared two major studies on the social
status of the first Christian generation in the Roman world: Gerd
Theissen's *The Social Setting of Pauline Christianity: Essays on
Corinth,*[10] and Wayne Meeks' *The First Urban Christians: The Social World of the Apostle Paul.* What is said of Theissen could be
said as well of Meeks, that "It would seem fair to characterize his
interests as more those of the social historian than those of the
sociologist."[11] Thus for Meeks the double task of the social historian, which he sets for himself, is to "try to discern the textures of
life in particular times and particular places" and "to describe the
life of the ordinary Christian within that environment."[12] For both
authors theory is helpful only insofar as it can illuminate the historical and social situation of early Christianity. Neither seems interested in the further step of verification of a theory per se for its
possible use in other cultural settings, as would be the social scientist. Thus Theissen and Meeks are rather typical of the biblical
scholars and historians of early Christianity who have entered the
field of social study of ancient texts: their focus and primary interest remains the world of early Christianity rather than a cross-
cultural application of social science models.

Because of the length and nature of Paul's two letters to Cor-

inth,[13] we have more information about that community than
about any other in Paul's world. Both books therefore deal with
the Pauline communities in general, but ultimately come to rest on
the Corinthian correspondence.

Using as a starting point the theme of the "wandering charismatic" which is developed further in his *Sociology of Early Palestinian Christianity,* Theissen's first chapter develops the supposed difference between that form of missionary activity and another
which he calls "community organizer." Here the issue is legitimation, focused on the question of community support for the missionary. Theissen distinguishes three types of basis for establishing the
legitimacy of one's claims to missionary authority and acceptance:
charismatic legitimation based on a certain lifestyle recognized as
appropriately ascetic; traditional legitimation based on origins of
teaching and authorization; functional legitimation based on observable achievements.

He suggests that the problem of Paul's self-support, raised
especially in 1 Corinthians 9, has to do with the favorable impression left on the Corinthians by other "charismatic" missionaries
whose voluntary poverty and dependence on community generosity seem among other factors to legitimate them in the eyes of the
local Christians. In addition, they can appeal to the best source,
probably the Jerusalem church, for their authorization: they seem
not only holy but in possession of impeccable credentials as well.
By contrast Paul insists that the missionary's support from the
community is a right, not an obligation. He appeals rather to the
effects of his ministry among them (functional), to his authorization by the risen Christ himself (traditional), and to his own type of
charismatic heroics, the preaching of the cross and the absurdity of
weakness (1 Cor 1). Thus Theissen argues that the question of the
apostle's material subsistence and the question of his theological
legitimacy are tightly bound to each other.

Both Theissen and Meeks give a great deal of attention to the
question of social stratification within the Pauline communities.
Theissen's second chapter focuses on the information that can be
gleaned about Corinthian Christians. On the basis of the evidence
available, Theissen argues that while most of the community come

from "the lower classes," by contrast there are some members from "the upper classes," mostly those who are sufficiently influential to have their names mentioned.

Theissen's exegesis of 1 Corinthians 1:26–29 proposes that while most of the Corinthian community are socially inconsequential, on the contrary some are capable of being singled out because of position by birth or status. Examples include Crispus of 1 Corinthians 1:14 who according to Acts 18:8 is an *archisynagōgos* or synagogue official; Stephanas of 1 Corinthians 1:16 whose "household" identifies him as well-to-do; Gaius of 1 Corinthians 1:14, also baptized by Paul, and suggested in Romans 16:23 as having a house large enough to host not only Paul but the whole community for its assembly; Prisca and Aquila, Paul's great merchant friends, who also host a house church in Romans 16:5; and especially Erastus, the city treasurer of Romans 16:23, who may be identified with the *aedile* (superintendent of public works) named in an inscription of approximately the same period still preserved near the theater of Corinth.

In addition, Pauline Christians engage in an extraordinary amount of travel over and above what we know to be direct missionary work: Prisca (Priscilla) and Aquila are connected with at least three different cities; Phoebe in Romans 16:1–2 seems about to undertake a journey with Paul's letter from Corinth to Rome; Chloe's people (1 Cor 1:11) have caught up with Paul elsewhere; Stephanas has arrived from Corinth to Ephesus with Fortunatus and Achaichus, possibly his slaves or freedmen, before the completion of 1 Corinthians (1 Cor 16:17), etc. Some of this travel may have been for the express purpose of delivering messages and letters to or from Paul, but more probably these are people moving about for their own business or personal reasons, from whose travel the churches profit to communicate with one another. When the information we have from Acts and the Pauline letters is laid out alongside what we know of the social and economic patterns of the cities in which these people lived, the conclusion which emerges is that the dominant evidence is in favor of rather high prosperity and social status for the Christians whose names we know. This of course says nothing about the silent majority.

Theissen carries this information in the direction of portraying the Corinthian community as test case for what may have been true in every early Christian community: that the social stratification of society in general carried over into the experience of Christians and came into conflict with the Christian ideal of fundamental equality before God. In other words, the Corinthian Christians, like Christians of any age, did not cease being affected by the variant values of their world all the while that they could proclaim the abolition of differences between Jew and Greek, slave and free, male and female in Christ (Gal 3:28; 1 Cor 12:13; Col 3:11)

The third and fourth chapters of *The Social Setting of Pauline Christianity* apply this assumption to the theological debates joined by Paul in 1 Corinthians 8, 10, and 11 about the question of meat sacrificed to idols and social discrimination at the Lord's supper. In 1 Corinthians 8 and 10 the issue is whether a Christian can: buy meat freely in the marketplace even though it may be surplus from the morning sacrifice in a nearby pagan temple; accept an invitation to dinner in a temple dining room rented for the occasion where such meat will certainly be served, and where the meal will probably begin or end with a sacrifice to the god; accept an invitation to dinner at the home of a pagan who may be serving meat that came from a temple sacrifice.

"The strong" seem to have had no problem with these cases, arguing with a certain philosophical sophistication that since idols are not real gods anyway, the whole question is irrelevant. "The weak" were not so easily convinced, but rather got caught up in cases of conscience and were scandalized when they saw "the strong" blithely munching on sacrificed meat with the rationalization that "everything is permitted" (1 Cor 8:4–8; 10:23–29). Paul's solution places priority on the integrity of the community: scandal to another believer is to be avoided (1 Cor 8:9–13; 10:25–29; see also Rom 14), and if there is any question of seeming to participate in idol worship, it cannot be allowed (1 Cor 10:14–22). Otherwise do what you think best.

That much is clear from the text. It has generally been assumed, however, that the difference of opinion between the strong and weak is purely a theological one, between persons with different approaches of conscience, or between Jewish and Gentile Christians. By contrast what Theissen suggests is that there is a connection between these differences and social stratification. Only the wealthy would have meat on their table frequently enough to be used to it as a regular part of their diet and nothing special. Poorer people who would have it only on special occasions would be more likely to raise such questions. Moreover, the wealthy are more likely to have had the kind of education which would permit an intellectual analysis and solution to the problem. The poorer members of the community with less education would be more inclined to see it as an either/or situation.

Thus according to Theissen Paul is dealing here with theological and ethical differences of interpretation which are characteristics of different social classes. His opinion is that when there is no conflict resulting in potential scandal, indeed anything is permitted. When however such conflict arises, the strong (the upper class people) are to accommodate their behavior to the weak (the lower class). This solution is typical of Paul's love ethic which places preservation of the bond of unity above either social or theological purity.

In 1 Corinthians 11:17–22 another social problem appears. There are factions which split the community and turn the celebration of the Lord's supper into a mockery. Some eat too much, some drink too much, and others go hungry. The love ethic has broken down. Theissen argues that this is not just a question of selfishness or lack of consideration on the part of some, but rather a reflection of social stratification as reflected in eating customs. He shows from convincing literary parallels about Greco-Roman dining habits that it was a familiar occurrence for those of upper class status to have or be served better food even in the presence of their social inferiors or dependents who had to make do with less food or poorer quality.

Evidently some in the Corinthian community have not quite caught on to the realistic implications of the Christian love ethic, but are continuing their ordinary discriminatory practices and indiscriminate imbibing even when meeting together for the solemn agape meal which will be climaxed by the eucharistic sharing of bread and cup in memory of Jesus' last meal with his disciples. What they have not realized and are doing violence to is the fact that "the sacramental act of the Lord's Supper is a symbolic accomplishment of social integration. From many people emerges a single entity."[14]

While Theissen has been criticized by Meeks and others for attempting to tie theological differences too closely to social status, his interpretations have on the whole been widely welcomed. They deserve to be received with the same caution as those of theologians, no less and no more. He has certainly done solid research and drawn provocative conclusions which cannot be ignored. He has demonstrated once again that theological conflicts do not exist independently of the social experiences and presuppositions of the persons involved.

In *The First Urban Christians,* Wayne Meeks more recently takes up many of the themes raised by Theissen and builds on his work and that of many others.[15] In an extensively documented book intended for the general reader, he portrays more thoroughly than Theissen the social and economic context of the Pauline communities. His first chapter on their urban environment recreates the world of the Greco-Roman city with its thriving commercial and intellectual life; its tradition of home rule by leading local families over against the pressures of Roman provincial administration; the effects of Roman military colonies in urban centers like Corinth or Philippi side by side with the traditional Greek population. The chapter highlights the way in which the cities grew progressively apart culturally from their surrounding villages and countryside as they entered the mainstream of a common urban culture, aesthetically Greek, administratively Roman.

The trade routes and commercial prosperity fostered the kind of geographical mobility for the business class which probably provided the context for much of the travel of Christians, as has already been mentioned. The upward social and economic mobility particularly of the freedman class provided a large group of the restless *nouveaux riches* very likely to be interested in new ideas and a new faith. The cities of the Pauline mission were port and market centers, military colonies and Roman provincial capitals. Many had large Jewish populations, whose synagogues according to Acts were the first centers for the missionary preaching of the apostles.

Meeks' second chapter again takes up the question of the

social level of Christians in Pauline communities, already discussed above in regard to Theissen. Meeks generally accepts and summarizes the findings of Theissen, Judge, and others who have done extensive work with the meager information provided in the New Testament texts, but he presents the relevant material clearly and in interesting fashion. The case of the collection for Jerusalem in 2 Corinthians 8 and 9 is pointed out as an instance in which the language of abundance and poverty is used figuratively, certainly, but also with the exception that the Corinthians and Macedonians are quite able to give of their financial abundance; indeed Paul seems to be playing the two groups off against each other in the hope that a little competitive feeling will produce better results (compare 2 Cor 8:2–3; 9:2–4)! Meeks draws attention to the comments by which Paul seems to have expected help from the Corinthians for his travel expenses from their city to the next on his itinerary (the usual meaning of *propempein* which is used here: 1 Cor 16:6,11; 2 Cor 1:16), quite the contrary of the blanket rejection he seems to make in 1 Corinthians 9:12–18 in regard to any kind of support from them.

The conclusions of Meeks' analysis of Christian social stratification generally agree with those of other recent scholars who have examined the evidence. With the exception of the extreme top and bottom of the social ladder, the Pauline communities are a cross-section of Greco-Roman urban society. There are no members of the senatorial or equestrian *ordines* and probably none of the lowest levels: unskilled laborers, peasants, and the habitually destitute. But all the intermediate levels are represented: slaves, freedmen and freedwomen, artisans and traders, small business people and merchants, people with extensive households who function as patrons, perhaps even an occasional prominent local family.

Meeks finds that those who can be singled out as most active in Paul's circles are those with high "status inconsistency" and consequent low "status crystallization," people whose "achieved status" acquired by taking advantage of new opportunities in their path is higher than their "attributed status" determined by birth. These are the people who are feeling the pressure between what they have been and what they could become, between what they would like to be and what the social stratification will still deny them. He then rightly asks whether these are the people likely to be most receptive to a new message of salvation, equality, and hope, or whether they simply stand out in any group because of the particular characteristics of their behavior. A question well worth asking, to which we will never know the answer for sure.

Meeks' third chapter examines four models from the social environment which may have influenced the shape of the Christian *ekklēsia*, the assembly or church: the household, the voluntary association or club, the synagogue, and the philosophical school. All have been described at least briefly at the beginning of this chapter, and the household will be taken up again in chapter 6 below. He then goes on to discuss the social function of boundaries in the Pauline community, using the categories of Victor Turner. The experience of social liminality is intended in Turner's schema as a transient and intermediate phase during a ritual of initiation, but is used here as a lasting state for those in eschatological preparedness. It leads to a warm, open, and egalitarian quality of relationship within the liminal group that Turner calls *communitas*. The boundaries which differentiate the group from the rest of society tend to reinforce their differentness. The stronger the boundaries, the stronger the inner sense of *communitas* and vice versa. While contrasting their own worldview to that of the outside world and therefore rejecting its structures, the group nevertheless necessarily creates its own alternative "anti-structures." Thus while insisting that Christian life is different and in some senses cut off from the world (e.g. the rejection of civil lawsuits for Christians in 1 Corinthians 6:1-6), nevertheless Paul insists on the maintenance of a decorum that would be acceptable even to outsiders (1 Cor 11:2-16; 14:23-35).

The language of separation in the Pauline writings reinforces the experience of liminality: while the insiders are the holy ones, those being saved, the others are unbelievers, the unrighteous, those who are perishing. There is not only a present social differentiation but a sequential one as well: those who were once enslaved to the powers of ignorance have now been set free in Christ. Since the body in any culture is an image of society, the treatment of the body in a culture will indicate the level of social control: tight control of purity regulations and bodily conduct is accompanied by a strict sense of in-group over against outsiders.[16] In Corinth different members of the community interpreted the boundaries differently with regard to eating meat sacrificed to idols (1 Cor 8 and 10); other differences of interpretation arose in regard to sexuality (1 Cor 6:12—7:7). With these questions as with those of community governing structure discussed in Meeks' fourth chapter, Paul's approach is to create strong boundaries of identity that are yet characterized by a certain freedom and flexibility in the application of rules.

The final chapters of Meeks' book pursue the function of ritual and patterns of belief in creating and sustaining the social world of Pauline Christians. The ritual of baptism is a "permanent threshold" through which the Christian enters a new order, a transition from darkness, ignorance, evil, the "dirty" world through the cleansing rite to light, knowledge, goodness, the "clean" new community. Divisions of social status are exchanged for unity in Christ, of which the ritual of eucharist is the living expression; hence Paul's refusal in 1 Corinthians 11:17–22 to tolerate violation of its symbolism.

Patterns of belief in Pauline teaching reinforce group identity and solidarity: the community is the body of Christ set off from the world by its paradoxical exaltation of the crucified one; its expectation of his imminent return puts it in a state of ongoing liminality in which it proclaims the beginnings of a transition from bondage to liberation, estrangement to reconciliation, guilt to justification. The status inconsistency already experienced by many Pauline Christians in their social status is transformed into a vision of common unity, but the tension of the inconsistency is not obliterated but rather transferred to the eschatological dimension of expectation. The Christian is status-inconsistent in a new way, between the old and new creations.

Conclusion

We have traced some of the social factors operative in the life of Paul and in the churches he founded. The evidence as illumined by recent scholarship indicates gatherings of people from across the social spectrum, with the exception of the very lowest levels and the highest aristocratic orders. In a cosmopolitan world, the Christian communities represented a fairly typical social mix, which in itself was probably somewhat untypical for a social or religious organization.

Those of unequal social status were to treat each other as brothers and sisters in the Lord. When husband and wife, master and slave, patron and client belonged to the same house church, they were to express their unity in Christ by sharing the same table and dealing with one another with equal consideration. What of the rest of their lives? Were the same unity and equality of status to carry over into their everyday lives? Such ideas were potentially subversive and were probably already in Paul's day sowing the seeds of future trouble.

Part III
MALE AND FEMALE: FAMILY STRUCTURES AND CHURCH ORGANIZATION

5
Charism, Authority and Structure

In the previous chapter we looked at the early Christian communities as part of their world, and at the social life of Christians and how it reflected the ordinary life around them. Except for a few remarks about styles of Christian leadership garnered from Theissen and Meeks, we have yet to focus on the internal structure of Christian communities in the Pauline churches and beyond. Before looking at those aspects of the New Testament in which family relationships came to be an important element, let us first examine the earlier period in which Christianity suggested an alternative to the family.

It is commonly accepted by scholars that 1 Corinthians 12—14 is to be taken seriously as Paul's articulation of his ideal vision of community: the mutual respecting of each other's spiritual gifts freely and responsibly exercised; the priority of love over all; the importance of prophecy; the necessity of maintaining order in the assembly. The picture is one of freedom and spontaneity in a relatively unstructured religious gathering that is, however, already beginning to establish recognized procedures (e.g. 1 Cor 12:18; 14:26–35). Definite and permanent kinds of authority are not yet invested in local leaders (though the beginnings of this kind of government may already be discernible in the overseers and deacons of Philippians 1:1 and the deacon Phoebe in Romans 16:1–2).

Because the itinerant missionary apostles are the initiators of Christian life in the diaspora, theirs is the earliest formulation of structures of authority. From the information to be gleaned predominantly from Acts and the Pauline letters, we can tentatively reconstruct a network of authority among Paul and his apostolic companions. This has been done most recently by Bengt Holmberg in *Paul and Power: The Structure of Authority in the Primitive Church as Reflected in the Pauline Epistles.*

The first part of the book assembles and interprets the data in three areas. The first area is Paul's relationship to the Jerusalem church. Despite Paul's protest in Galatians 1 and 2 that he received the gospel he preaches not from human authority but directly from the risen Christ, a close reading of even that passage reveals in Paul a certain deference to those in Jerusalem with legitimate ties to the historical Jesus: "I laid out privately to those who were qualified the gospel that I preach to the Gentiles, lest I go or had gone somehow off on the wrong track" (Gal 2:3). Holmberg concludes that for Paul the officials in Jerusalem have "status authority" in virtue of their unique qualifications. Paul submits to their authority in two ways: by seeking and accepting their authorization at the Jerusalem summit meeting (also described in Acts 15), and by making the collection of funds in the Greek churches and turning it over to the Jerusalem church. Paul does this, Holmberg argues, not out of charity but as a matter of ecclesiology, as a demonstration of the deference he felt was owed by Gentile Christians to the "mother church."

The second area of data interpretation is the network of relationships among Paul and his co-workers.[1] From eighty to one hundred (depending on how one interprets certain passages) are named in the Pauline letters and Acts in some kind of cooperative association in ministry. It is usually only through careful analysis of the language that patterns and structures can be detected, i.e. Titus (2 Cor 8:6) and Apollos (1 Cor 16:12) are "urged" while Timothy is "sent" (1 Thes 3:2; 1 Cor 4:17; Phil 2:19); Phoebe the deacon is "commended" as a benefactor (Rom 16:1–2), while Barnabas is a respected leader, a traveling companion and partner of Paul but never his subordinate. In fact, Holmberg speculates that Paul may originally have been an assistant of Barnabas before striking out independently (see Acts 11:24–26).

The third area of interpretation of Pauline authority is in the local churches founded by Paul. Holmberg finds that here Paul has personal authority because of the power of his own person and his acknowledged holiness. He also has procedural or functional authority by virtue of what he represents. As "their" founder and apostle he bears divine (though certainly not absolute) authority, and does not hesitate to wield it when a situation moves in a different direction than he would judge best.

Charism and Office

The more difficult issue in regard to authority in the local churches is the extent to which local leadership had already in Paul's day developed into what can later be clearly defined as "office," that is, "permanent acknowledged functions in local churches filled by stable groups of persons who lead and serve and take responsibility for their congregations in different ways, in some cases even having a designation or title and some form of material support."[2] Holmberg's conclusion is that even though according to this description the function is not yet fully developed, still we can rightly speak of such "office" in the Pauline churches.

It has been customary among early church historians since the turn of the century to juxtapose or play off against one another as dialectically opposed forces the two factors of "charism" and "office." In this way of thinking "charism" is free, unstructured, prophetic leadership which derives its authority from the inspiration of the Spirit, and responds in an *ad hoc* manner to needs as they arise. "Office" then is permanent, stable leadership by designated individuals, founded on juridically constituted authority which is regularly transmitted in a hierarchical succession. Stereotypically put, charism means freedom and spontaneity; office means stability and continuity, and ultimately the suppression of charism under the weight of its authority. Thus the two factors represent opposite and irreconcilable poles, one of which was swallowed up and destroyed by the other in the course of early church history. The charismatic church would then be represented by the authentic Pauline letters, especially Romans, Galatians, and 1 and 2 Corinthians, the official church by the later, or deutero-Pauline letters, Colossians, Ephesians, 1 and 2 Timothy and Titus, and by such other later New Testament books as 1 and 2 Peter, James, and Jude, most of which seem to present the picture of a more stabilized church structure, sometimes referred to in this literature as "early Catholicism."

More recently this historical interpretation has been called into question as simplistic, and Holmberg's conclusion that one can properly speak of "office" already in the Pauline churches is typical of this trend. If "office" is already present in Paul's churches, it is equally true that "charism" does not disappear in the later, more institutionalized church of the second and third centuries, since some of the most hierarchical authority figures of that period, e.g. Ignatius of Antioch and Cyprian of Carthage, consider themselves "charismatics" who possess the spirit of prophecy and live according to its inspiration. In short, though there is a definitely traceable development of institutionalization that takes place in the early church and is already discernible in the New Testament, it cannot be blamed for the demise of charism.[3] The explanation of later developments is more complex. How then to explain it?

Sociology and Authority

Here is where sociological theory steps in. The second part of Holmberg's book builds on the exegetical conclusions of the first to elucidate the structure of authority in the earliest years of the church by means of the theories of the well-known sociologist of religion, Max Weber. Weber understands authority as power to cause another to assent, not out of constraint but out of conviction. He distinguishes three types of authority or "legitimate domination": charismatic, due to the exceptional characteristics of the person and/or a claim to supernatural revelation; traditional, based on established procedures and accepted legitimacy; rational-legal, resting on belief in the legality of rules and the rights of those who exercise authority under those rules.

What Weber documented and formulated into theory some years ago was the development of charismatic leadership into institutional leadership, the process whereby charism becomes traditionalized, rationalized, or both—the "routinization" of charism, as he called it. For Weber and for many church historians, this development is a lamentable decline, even though probably inevitable if the group is to continue. Weber's observations apply to any social or religious movement which begins with the enthusiastic response of followers to a visionary leader. They are still helpful for understanding the origins of Christianity and of sub-groups within it throughout history, such as religious orders.

A problem arises when a negative value judgment about the development from charismatic to traditional/legal group, from sect to institution, prevails. Then there is a pristine Christianity which existed only for a brief period, perhaps one generation—that of Jesus and Paul. Once the powers of routinization and institutionalization set to work, the original impetus is diluted into something of secondary value: the time of the later New Testament and all subsequent generations, punctuated by periodic renewal movements which eventually suffer the same fate. It's a pretty bleak picture of religious history.

Holmberg takes up Weber's theory, applies it to the changes taking place in the Pauline churches, and suggests an alternative interpretation of the development from sect to institution. Rather than speaking of the routinization of charism, Holmberg proposes to understand the process as the transformation of charismatic leadership and structure into other types. This is especially relevant if the charismatic authority himself/herself is not the victim of institutionalization, but rather the initiator, as Holmberg finds Paul to be. When the charism seeks institutional manifestation for the sake of stability, order, and continuity, a new phase in the life of the movement is underway, neither better nor worse, but necessary for survival. The effects of this institutionalizing phenomenon move in two directions. First, there is more social control and less general freedom. Second, a different kind of freedom is created: freedom from the pressure and ambiguity of living in an unstructured world, and as a result further capacity for self-governed action.

Holmberg would describe the apostolic church as an institutionalized charismatic movement, that is, a movement begun through the inspiration of a dynamic leader whose very person commanded authority and whose claim to revelation was compelling, a movement which subsequently followed the inevitable laws of nature for such groups by evolving structures and more permanent types of authority which responded to the ongoing need for ordering in a continuing existence. In the process, the charism is not lost, but transformed into different shapes and manifestations.

Weber's work has been criticized on minor points and on some of his interpretations of the overall implications of his theory. Its main lines remain valid. Holmberg's careful analysis and critique of Weber are an important contribution to the understanding of early Christianity. Not everyone will agree with his exegetical conclusions, especially his excessive dependence on Acts as historically reliable, at times even against Paul. Those who envision Paul as champion of unstructured freedom over against later Christian institutionalists will not approve of his attempt to demonstrate a well-ordered authority network in the first Christian generation. But here is a scholar who portrays the transition to institutionalized structure as beginning much earlier than many have thought, and he argues his point well, not out of denominational partisanship but from textual data and sociological theory.

What were some of the factors which prompted this institutionalizing development in the next generation after Paul? This will be the subject of the next chapter.

6
The Household Code
and Its Implications

One of the characteristics of many of the later books of the New Testament written in letter form is the tendency to encourage more definite structures of church life. This has already been mentioned in the previous chapter. The descriptions of qualifications for bishops, deacons, widows, and presbyters in 1 Timothy 3:1–13 and 5:3–22 and Titus 1:5–9 are good examples which indicate early forms of established leadership roles. There is a particular literary form in this category which has recently been the subject of much interest from the perspective of social setting: the household code. This form consists of sets of mutually reciprocal duties among categories of people in the extended patriarchal household: usually husbands and wives, masters and slaves, parents and children. Examples are: Ephesians 5:21—6:9, Colossians 3:18—4:1 and 1 Peter 2:13—3:8. Note that not all passages contain exhortations for all six groups.

Recall what was said in chapter 4 about the strong need for ordering in the Greco-Roman world, the importance of authority figures as guardians and preservers of that order, and the centrality of the extended family as the basic unit of society, after which, according to many ancient philosophers, the other basic social unit, the city-state, is modeled. It is time now to turn our attention to the structuring of this extended patriarchal family, its literary expression in the household code, and the significance of these social concepts for Christian life in the late first and early second centuries.

To know the origin of the household code is to know something of its history, social setting, and intention. Unfortunately, there is no agreement on its origins, and it represents a way of thinking that is very familiar in the ancient world. A book by David Balch, *Let Wives Be Submissive: The Domestic Code in 1 Peter,* explores the possible origins and function of the household code particularly in 1 Peter in a way that highlights the social setting and real circumstances behind its use in one New Testament letter.

Balch's exploration of the origins of the household code leads him to reject prior theories of its beginnings in Jewish ethical teaching or philosophers contemporary to the New Testament writers. Rather, he finds it to be a literary theme traceable at least as far back as Plato and Aristotle, though it was probably already old in their day. There are two familiar and related topics for philosophical discourse traceable at least that far back: On Household Management and On the Constitution, that is, on the essential and ideal ingredients for both domestic and political prosperity and harmony. Discussion of these interrelated topics continues through the philosophical treatises and ethical manuals of the Hellenistic period and on into Roman times.

The two topics are interrelated precisely because of the concept articulated by Plato and followed by many others including the first century Jewish philosopher Philo—that the household is a microcosm of the state, or, put differently, the state is a macrocosm of the household. Thus maintenance of order in one is integral to maintenance of order in the other; subversion in one means inevitable subversion in the other. The quality of harmony in the state is then intimately dependent on the harmony of the family. Disruption of family patterns means disruption of the political process and vice versa (compare the nineteenth and twentieth century fear that the granting of equal rights to women is injurious to the family). The patriarchal family head, the *paterfamilias* in Roman terminology, cannot govern in the civil sphere if he cannot govern in the domestic sphere (compare the church leader in 1 Timothy 3:4–5 who cannot manage a church if he cannot manage his household).

In many of these passages, the same triple dyadic pattern is present as in the New Testament household codes: husband-wife, master-slave, parent-child.

It is interesting to note that Aristotle objected to the comparison of household and state in regard to the exercise of authority, for he considered the style of household authority too harsh and severe to be extrapolated to the political sphere. While in practice he was probably correct, in theory the Platonic association and interrelationship of the two continued to exercise tremendous influence in the literature of several centuries.

Implicit in this association, of course, is the assumption that good order requires a hierarchical pattern of dominance and submission not only with regard to children and slaves, but also with regard to wives. While the legal treatment of women varied from region to region and from generation to generation in the ancient world, never in Greco-Roman or Jewish society did women enjoy full legal status. They were always in some way under the protection and dominance of male authority. The actual exercise of this dominance may have taken the severe form of the right of life and death on the part of the *paterfamilias* in early republican Rome, or the apparently extensive independence enjoyed by women under Roman law to conduct their own business, legal, and social transactions during the years of the empire. But women's status as legal persons never equaled that of men.

While philosophers disputed whether or not men and women had the same nature and the same capacity for virtue, the notion that the public domain belonged properly to men and the domestic domain to women was prevalent and considered the ideal. Exceptions were notable, scarce, and often legendary. As independent as some upper-class women of imperial Rome may have been, none ever held government positions. In spite of good evidence to the contrary, the ideal virtuous woman proposed by male writers was shy, retiring, and happy to remain secluded at home, occupied with domestic management and weaving.[1]

Even those philosophers who argued for equality of nature between men and women seem to have seen no contradiction between affirming equality of nature and inequality of social roles. This contradiction was apparently not widely recognized until modern times. Wives, slaves, and children are the three groups in the Roman world from whom submission was required. And if the dominance-submission pattern was not really questioned between men and women, it is not surprising that the *institution* of slavery (as distinct from its abuse) was not widely questioned on philosophical or humanitarian grounds, either. What becomes noticeably different in the New Testament codes is the exhortation to *mutual* submission on the part of all (e.g. Eph. 5:21).

Function of the Code in 1 Peter

The household code of 1 Peter 2:13—3:8 has several peculiarities. First, it is introduced by an exhortation to everyone to submit to all legitimate political authority as to God (2:13–17). Second, parents and children are completely lacking, and the order of the remaining two sets is reversed. Third, there is no exhortation to masters, and the verses devoted to slaves are expanded into a commentary on the sufferings of Christ that is explicitly patterned after parts of the suffering servant passage of Isaiah 53, seeming to tell slaves to bear all suffering patiently in memory of the suffering Christ. Fourth, the exhortation to wives goes so far as to encourage *obedience* to husbands (3:6) after the example of Sarah to Abraham, a doubtful exegesis of the intention of Genesis 18:12. Fifth, the beginning of the exhortation to wives (3:1) leaves a telltale sign of possible social conflict: the virtuous submission of wives to their husbands may bring about the husbands' conversion to the faith.

Balch draws on the comparative evidence of Greek mystery cults, and the accusations leveled indiscriminately against them, against Judaism, and against Christianity as well, of secret nocturnal meetings full of immorality, of disruption of familial concord by encouragement of individual conversions from either sex and any legal status without approval of the proper patriarchal authority. These independent decisions of conversion naturally implied further ongoing independent activity (attendance at meetings and worship services and daily personal prayer) which was seen by many as a serious threat to the stability of the family. Disparity of worship within a household was already a problem. Disparity of worship between husband and wife was crucial; one of the ideals proposed by the writers on marriage and household management was that, no matter what gods a young woman was accustomed to worship in her parents' house, she should forsake them at marriage and worship only those of her husband. Encouraging wives and slaves to think independently and accept the authority of someone other than the male householder was indeed subversion of domestic order and therefore of civil order, a sufficient cause for resentment and persecution.

At this point let us recall some of the impressions we can gather of the earlier Pauline communities, where the family unit is the body of Christ, the community with its many members, where authority is claimed by apostles, prophets, and teachers (1 Cor 12:28), not by heads of households. There the Christian community really functions as an *alternative* to the household. Paul will sometimes speak in patriarchal terms (Phil 2:22; 1 Thes 2:11; 1 Cor 4:14–15) since this is a familiar idiom in his society, but he does not go about setting up communities governed by the type of hierarchical paternal authority typical of the household of the day. Nevertheless, the power of the apostle vis-à-vis his congregation is a definite authority over persons who also belong to households in which the patriarchal head may or may not also be Christian (read 1 Corinthians 7:12–16,20–24 on wives and slaves from this perspective). When he is not, patterns of suspicion and resentment are no doubt present.

Balch proposes that it is in answer to just such a situation that the author of 1 Peter writes his household code. It aims to show that in every possible respect, Christians conform to the expectations of society: slaves are humble and obedient even when unjustly punished; wives are chaste, simple, and submissive. Their faith need not be a threat to the social status quo. The household code in 1 Peter therefore functions as a defensive apologetic answer to slanderous accusation of misconduct. If Christianity is accused of disrupting the social order, especially through conversions of wives and slaves, it is those very groups who are in the strongest terms urged to live exemplary lives in all other respects. The code is a document which can be cited to show outsiders that Christians really stand for order, whatever contrary rumors may be circulating. At the same time, it instructs Christians, especially wives and slaves of pagan households and masters, who are in the most vulnerable position, how to behave in order to appease those in power. Hope is even held out that the good example of Christian wives may convert their husbands, though that was probably too much to hope for in the case of slaves in regard to their masters.

The Church as Household

Another and more extensive recent study of 1 Peter approaches the form and function of the letter somewhat differently. John H. Elliott's *A Home for the Homeless: A Sociological Exegesis of 1 Peter, Its Situation and Strategy* attempts to develop a method called by the author "sociological exegesis." By combining interpretations from the historical-critical method and models from the social sciences, Elliott seeks to correlate the literary, sociological, and theological aspects of the text as well as its intended impact, which he calls the author's "strategy."

Elliott calls attention to some of the peculiar language of 1 Peter which situates it in its contemporary world, where the present existence of Christians is called their *paroikia* (1:17), and they themselves are referred to as *paroikoi* (2:11) and *parepidēmoi* (1:1; 2:11). In the legal terminology of the ancient Greek world, the *paroikos* (Latin equivalent: *peregrinus*) is a resident alien permanently without rights of citizenship because of status by birth, just as citizenship in a city is restricted to those born into families with the legal status of citizen. The *parapidēmos* is one with even less status, a visiting stranger with no permanent habitation in the political entity. Thus the associations of impermanence, transiency, and exile are attached to the terms.

Elliott goes further in attempting to situate the actual social setting of the letter. The addressees of 1:1 belong to central and northern Asia Minor (present-day Turkey), a largely rural area though not without its urban centers. He calls attention to the rural imagery used in the letter (e.g. 1:22–24; 2:25; 5:2–4) and draws upon available historical evidence of the disintegrating situation of the rural laboring classes of Asia Minor to suggest that the language of temporary residential status may be more than figurative, that a real social situation of legal contingency and increasing eco-

nomic hardship leads the author to use the exile theme as a way of
understanding the community's theological status as comparable
to its civil status, an idea already in common use (e.g. Phil 3:20;
Heb 13:14). At the same time, typical language of urban life, like
Paul's *ekklēsia* (assembly of citizens) and *politeuma* (citizenship in
a political entity—cf. Phil 3:20), is notably absent. He therefore
concludes that the predominant audience of 1 Peter comes from
the rural peasant class.

Elliott then introduces a series of characteristics of religious
sects as compiled by cross-cultural observation and analysis according to social science method: tension with the external world, disillusionment with the social situation, definite internal procedures
and expectations, voluntary membership, egalitarian ideals, and
future-oriented stance. The sect's biggest tension is between its
open mission orientation, born of the conviction of the rightness
and goodness of its positions, and the necessity to close out the
external world to preserve internal cohesion. The sociological result of conflict is the necessity to reinforce group identity and
cohesion for the sake of the survival and health of the movement.

Since the days of Max Weber early Christianity has been studied sociologically under the category of the sect. Thus Elliott argues that most of the above characteristics can be seen in 1 Peter.
In the face of persecution, clearly alluded to in the letter (3:13–17;
4:12–19; 5:10), the author's strategy is to reinforce group cohesion
by stressing internal coherence over against the external world.
The readers are encouraged not to become but to remain what
they already are, socially as well as theologically: resident aliens.
By not playing on the "heavenly home" theme as do Philippians
3:20 and Hebrews 13:14, the author of 1 Peter reveals the link with
the readers' social-legal status: they are not to "put on" a notion of
impermanence for the sake of eschatology; rather, they are to
make sense, in light of their faith, of the real situation they face.
There is no escapism here.

Within this internally coherent community, the operant model
is the household, not because of the church's assimilation to societal models (as argued by Balch), but as an alternative household
of God which operates not by human standards but by divine ones.
In support of this interpretation is the recurrent household lan-

guage of the letter. The community is to be built into a spiritual household (2:5), the household of God (4:17), in which all are house servant-stewards (4:10), and husbands live together with their wives in domestic harmony (3:7). In the household code, the usual word for slaves, *douloi,* is replaced by *oiketai,* specifically house slaves. Though it may not be clear in the various English translations, each of the passages cited above uses in Greek some form or compound of *oikos,* house or household.

Elliott therefore argues that 2:5–10, whose language of priesthood and sacrifice is usually understood as figurative appropriation of Jewish worship into the beginnings of a notion of Christian cultic sacrifice, is not meant to be cultic language at all, but rather a movement from temple to household as the model of the Christian structure of worship.[2]

Here we must again recall what has been said previously about the importance of the household as the basic social unit. The city and the empire are structured along similar lines; the emperor is *pater patriae,* father of the fatherland; his vast administrative network of civil servants is his *familia,* and patriotism means loyalty to the patriarchal system. In Elliott's view the church of 1 Peter does not copy all this, but rather provides an alternative in recognizable form, the household of God which operates according to radically different principles.

In the household code of 1 Peter, therefore, slaves unexpectedly are mentioned first and longest for a theologial reason, because they best exemplify the household concept (not because their conversion is the biggest public relations problem as Balch would have it). But the slaves of the code are not merely literal slaves. They are the paradigm of all Christians and especially of those who suffer. The wives of pagan husbands are not only literally so, but also symbols of the gentleness, patience, and submission by which Christians will be accepted by pagans and win them over. The crisis faced by the community is not in Elliott's view one of blatant and open persecution but rather the result of more subtle kinds of pressure and oppression which Christians are experiencing within their daily lives and even in the heart of their families. Reinforcement of the internal cohesion of the community provides the security its members need to persevere in faith and hope—a home for the homeless where they can reaffirm their true identity and create kinship ties that go deeper than blood relationship.

Elliott's reconstruction of the situation and strategy of 1 Peter is a much vaster understanding than the work of Balch. It is an enormous step forward toward an understanding of the letter, and has been generally well received. Criticisms usually center around three areas. First, the missionary strategy, the other side of sectarian cohesiveness, is neglected, and it too must be taken into account for a full understanding of the letter; the author is not closed into his own world. Second, the interpretation of the social situation is pushed too far: such rural imagery as appears in 1 Peter is commonplace and does not necessarily indicate an agrarian setting; the *paroikos* language must be seen in the context of other examples of figurative literary use of legal terminology without indication of corresponding social status, e.g. Paul's frequent description of himself as a slave which in no way suggests for him the legal condition of slavery. Such figurative use of legal terms is also well known from non-Christian sources of the period.

The third criticism deals with the whole method involved. Elliott sets out to produce an analysis that interweaves sociological with historical, literary, and exegetical method. He succeeds well in the use of various methods side by side, but not in combining and melding them, particularly the social sciences, the inclusion of which is the new frontier. The introduction of sociological data and analysis does not in itself produce a "sociological exegesis." Nevertheless, Elliott has put forth a bold attempt that breaks new ground in the use of social science method in the study of early Christian literature and life.

Social Science Becomes Social Critique

The interpretations of Balch and Elliott open up new possibilities for situating 1 Peter as well as other later New Testament writings within their social contexts and early Christian history and theology. What neither writer has taken into account are the implications of the adoption of the household by Christian groups already near the end of the first century as the primary model of Christian relationship. Whether the motive was social adaptation to enhance acceptance and conversion as argued by Balch, or the creation of the alternative household of God as proposed by Elliott, the effect is the same. The household structure is canonized, and with it the patriarchal pattern of dominance and submission which it implies.

Fatherhood becomes the model for the exercise of authority in the church, and the submission of wives and obedience of slaves and children the models for response to that authority. The household codes convey a deeply challenging invitation to the *loving* exercise of authority and obedience, but their proponents do not question the appropriateness of the patriarchal structure itself as a model for Christian relationship.

Theissen and Troeltsch before him speak of "love-patriarchalism" as the foundational ethic of early Christian communities. Under this concept equality of status in Christ belongs to all regardless of social status. But "in the political and social realm class-specific differences were essentially accepted, affirmed, even religiously legitimated."[3] The difference for Christians was the emphasis on mutual love as the mode of relationship within the given hierarchically structured society. For Balch and Theissen the conflict was created by the tension between two principles difficult to harmonize: patriarchy and equality of freedom in Christ. For Elliott that tension seems to resolve into the love-patriarchalism of a community that sees itself as the household of God.

But is the tension really resolved so easily? This assumption of early Christians' willing acceptance of a social theology of inequality is being questioned from the perspective of liberation critique, most recently by Elisabeth Schüssler Fiorenza, *In Memory of Her: A Feminist Theological Reconstruction of Christian Origins*. By viewing early Christianity as a *social* reality, Fiorenza is able to utilize a formidable amount of the social history and social science research into Christian origins to challenge centuries-long assumptions about the inherent patriarchalism of the tradition from its earliest years. For both Theissen and Fiorenza, the teaching and attitude of Jesus represent an alternative approach open to the equality of all under the sole authority of God. While Theissen would see the principle of love-patriarchalism already operative in the Pauline churches and Paul's own teachings, Fiorenza posits its

Christian beginnings only in the later New Testament writings, though she concedes that the language of fatherhood sometimes used by Paul (e.g. 1 Cor 4:15,17,21; 2 Cor 11:2–3; Phil 2:22) opens the way toward the subsequent return of Christians to the patriarchal model.

Fiorenza suggests status dissonance—the anomaly of possessing different levels of status at the same time—as motivation for the large numbers of women who joined religious groups and private clubs, synagogues and Christian assemblies. In the household they were structurally and legally inferior even though as wives or widows of the well-to-do they may have exercised a great deal of independence and authority over others. Private associations and minority religious groups not organized along the lines of the dominant social structure gave them the experience of freedom and respect that they had tasted but that was officially denied to them elsewhere.

The Pauline churches would have provided just such an experience, in which the reality of individual charisms was affirmed regardless of legal status, ethnic origins, or sex (Gal 3:28), even though in specific local situations Paul may not have been as totally consistent with his principles as some would have liked (e.g. 1 Cor 11:2–16; 14:34–35 if this passage is authentically Pauline). Later New Testament writers see patriarchalism as a social and political necessity for the maintenance of order. Ephesians, Colossians, and the pastoral epistles use the household codes to reinforce the patriarchal model within the community itself; 1 Peter may use it for external propaganda (Balch) but also for internal use (Elliott) because notions of equality are seen as a threat to the social order itself—an idea that is at least as old as Plato and Aristotle.

Liberation social critique reaffirms the primary Christian egalitarian vision as reconstructed by social science method and social history. It calls for the re-creation of an alternative social model which will respect that original vision and call together a community of mutuality, in which patterns of domination and submission are overcome by love and full personhood is able to be realized by all.

Fiorenza and others[4] represent the cutting edge of the merger of social science method and liberation theology, one of the important directions in which social study of the Bible is moving. The social scientists and social historians can highlight their findings in regard to the diversity and adaptability of early Christian structures and ideals. It is then up to biblical theologians to interpret these findings and their significance for our life today. If biblical religion's prophetic proclamation of freedom and liberation to the suffering and oppressed is to mean anything beyond historical data, it must take on this added dimension.

Part IV
USING
SOCIAL SCIENCE
MODELS

7
A Further Look
at Models in Action

In the previous chapters, reference has been made to social science models and theorists, and we have seen how some biblical scholars have used them. We have looked at the use of Mediterranean anthropology by B. Malina in chapter 2, and at the application of models by A. Saldarini, J. Gager, G. Theissen, and R. Horsley in chapter 3, and by B. Holmberg and J. Elliott in chapter 5. But much attention has also been given to elements of social description that enable the general reader better to reconstruct the world of the New Testament. Since the first edition of this book appeared, much more has been done on social science application to New Testament texts. In this chapter we will first look at the work of two biblical scholars who have attempted to formulate sociological or anthropological approaches that would be helpful for New Testament study. Later we shall see how models can be applied to a single biblical book in its entirety.

Interrogating the Text

H.C. Kee, in *Knowing the Truth: A Sociological Approach to New Testament Interpretation,* gives a good introduction in his first two chapters to pertinent social theory, especially in the area of sociology of knowledge. The third chapter, "Interrogating the Text: A Sociological Proposal for Historical Interpretation," seeks to raise all the crucial questions that must be asked of a text in order to surface the constitutive elements of the symbolic worldview shared by author and intended audience.[1]

The questions fall into seven categories which, taken together, form a good working list with which to approach any text large enough to yield sufficient information. First are boundary questions, which ask about insiders and outsiders, authority and means of maintaining boundaries, self-perception of insiders, and time-space frame. Second are authority questions that ask about the function of power and leadership. Third are status and role questions that look at bases for classification among persons. Fourth are ritual questions that ask how rituals are performed, by whom, and with what assigned meaning. Fifth are literary questions with social implications: the social effects of literary genre, strategy, and operative canon. Sixth are questions about group functions: community dynamics, group tensions, and means of maintaining group identity. The final set of questions concerns two concepts from the sociology of knowledge: symbolic universe and the social construction of reality. These are questions of shared group self-understanding and interpretations of time and space, perceptions of God and the universe, and the use of symbols. The final chapter of the book discusses the theological notion of covenant as formative of social identity in the New Testament.

The analysis of a full text from these perspectives can yield fruitful results. Kee is aware that not every ancient text will contain information in all areas; in fact, most will not. Yet he maintains that this set of questions must continue to be asked if we are to gain insight into the interpretive social world of the early Christians. In the remainder of the book Kee uses the concept of covenant as an interpretive key for understanding New Testament social identity. *Knowing the Truth* is a good example of the approach that seeks to let models arise from the material at hand rather than appropriate them directly from social science.

A previous example is W. Meeks, *First Urban Christians,* discussed above in chapter 4. But whereas Meeks borrows eclectically from social science theorists where a concept seems to fit the text, Kee argues for beginning not with models at all but with leading questions that will let the interpretation arise from the text itself.

Using this method can be very productive, especially in a working group or class setting, for it compels the reader to look for signals that are often passed over when only theological clues are sought.

Critics would cite the lack of an articulated theoretical framework on which to build observations, and the subsequent danger of being unconscious of our own implicit assumptions. Thus we run the risk of assuming uncritically that what we see in a text, informed by our own social construction of reality, is the same as what ancient readers or participants would have seen. Nevertheless, Kee and others like him provide good working tools for the attempt to comprehend the world of the New Testament.

An Exercise in Models

Quite a different approach is taken by B. Malina in *Christian Origins and Cultural Anthropology: Practical Models for Biblical Interpretation*. Malina presents his work as a "big picture" effort that provides tentative theoretical generalizations rather than collections of detailed data. He forewarns that a detailed fit for every situation is not the goal, but rather that "here readers are urged to stretch the models to their limit, to draw further conclusions, to multiply correlations, and to come to grips with the dimensions of the models undeveloped in this book" (pp. iii–v).

After an introductory discussion of basic terms, Malina takes up Mary Douglas' group-grid model, a complex proposal for understanding societies that would require careful reading of her essay on "Cultural Bias" to comprehend completely.[2] Basically, as interpreted by Malina, "grid" is "the degree of socially constrained adherence" given by persons in a group to the received symbol systems. It is "the measurement of fit between socially shared conceptions and human experiences," or the degree to which socially mediated expectations and experience match (p. 13). If one imagined a vertical line indicator, those societies in which there was a high match between expectation and experience, in which socially shared concepts received a high trust rating, would be "high grid"; those in which such consistency was not strong would be "low grid."

On an imaginary horizontal scale, the degree of "group" can be plotted; that is, "the degree of social pressure exerted upon an individual or some subgroup to conform to the demands of the larger society" (p. 13). If the grid (vertical) measure is combined with the group (horizontal) measure, the result is a square graph on which any society can theoretically be located, and in which the societies in each quadrant will have their own characteristic attitudes toward the basic elements that constitute a symbolic universe: purity, ritual, personal identity, body, sin, cosmology, and suffering and misfortune.

Thus weak group/high grid at upper left, with little social pressure to conform but a high correlation between values and outcome, tends to emphasize a pragmatic and individualist ethic: enter mainstream U.S. culture. At lower left, weak group/low grid culture has neither great pressure toward social conformity nor great consistency between expectations and experience. It will be characterized by revolt against institutions, pessimism about power structures, and individualistic egalitarianism. Typical residents of this quadrant would include U.S. adolescents, "flower children," and perhaps the community behind the gospel of John (see chapter 8, below).

On the right side of the quadrant, strong group/high grid society maintains tight group control and the members of the group optimistically share the common vision. Examples might be the elites of the Roman empire, the Vatican, successful business corporations, or the Soviet Union before the recent collapse of communism. At lower right, strong group/low grid society keeps the concern for control of boundaries and group cohesion and conformity, but with the perception that life is unstable and threatened from without. It can reflect the experience of the underside of an oppressive society. The social experience behind most of the New Testament would fall here, where group belonging takes precedence over individualism (see the discussion of dyadic personality in chapter 2) and the social construction of reality is being reexamined in the light of new data.

This brief description of Douglas' schema and Malina's adaptation of it does not really do justice to its complexitiy and flexibility, but gives an introduction to its possibilities. Remember that the schema functions like a four-sided graph on which positions can be plotted in two dimensions (see chart in Malina, pp. 14–15). Thus no position is absolute, but always comparative, as if on a sliding scale.

The group/grid schema is the foundation upon which the rest of the book builds. While working with this for several chapters, Malina step by step interjects new categories and artfully blends them in, not under the image of construction of a building, but of a game played on several fields or courts, each with its own boundaries and rules—perhaps an appeal to his primary undergraduate audience as in his earlier book, *The New Testament World*.

Chapter 4 introduces the generalized symbolic media (GSM) of social interaction, as drawn from T. Parsons:[3] commitment, influence, power, and inducement, and suggests creative ways to discover how each is at work in some of the social exchanges of contemporary life and the New Testament. Ways are given in which the GSM might function within Douglas' group/grid structure.

The next chapter adds yet another level adapted primarily from M. Sahlins:[4] the three types of reciprocity interactions. Generalized reciprocity is oriented to the needs of the other without specific expectation of return. Balanced reciprocity is oriented at the same time both to the needs of the other and of the self, specific in its expectation of return, and thus focused on the exchange itself as symbolic communication. Negative reciprocity is oriented to the needs of the self (understood as individual or extended social self), and is intended as a transaction in which the self will get the better deal, e.g. forms of dishonesty and fraud. It is an interesting exercise to apply these categories to many forms of exchange in the New Testament: the miracles and preaching of Jesus; apostolic preaching and ministry; Paul's collection for the Jerusalem church, etc. Malina suggests (p. 105) applying the norms of reciprocity to the ten commandments with the question about who is the neighbor or the "thou" envisioned in social context. What is praiseworthy with an insider may not be with the outsider, etc. This discussion leads to forms of non-reciprocal interaction, centricity of collectivity for the sake of mutual benefit; and of agglomeration, overworked centricity in which the GSM are so heavily concentrated that only the elite benefit.

Chapter 6 deals with the social construction of norms, standards, customs, and laws, all the while working this new layer of categories into the group/grid structure. A helpful final section (pp. 131–138) applies the material of this chapter to the Pauline writings and especially to Paul's understanding of the law.

Chapters 7 and 8 explore the role of the symbolic action of ritual and ceremony, and of the symbolic language of discourse and narrative. The latter builds on the work of H. White on the creative process of historical reconstruction.[5] The final chapter attempts to apply as much as possible of the multi-layered model built up throughout the book to the case of fasting in the New Testament. After sketching how fasting would be valued differently in the four quadrants of the group/grid schema, Malina examines, for example, how fasting establishes group and personal boundaries, communicates messages of social interaction according to the GSM, and is a refusal to reciprocate according to accepted social modes. Some of the specific New Testament passages about fasting are then examined according to these perspectives.

This brief summary touches only on the highlights of a fascinating book. Malina says at the beginning that he is engaging in intellectual "kitbashing," a term borrowed from model railroading, where it means taking pieces of different models and combining them in new ways. There is no claim here to be a study of the various social science theories drawn upon. Rather, they are borrowed and changed as they are interwoven into new patterns.

It is clear that for the author this kind of "kitbashing" is meant to be both enlightening and enjoyable at the same time. As with the set of questions posed by Kee, so these models can be fruitfully worked with, especially in a study group or classroom context. The models are presented at a high level of abstraction. Because so many conceptual structures are introduced so quickly, the book is not easy reading. It is not a text to be read through, but one to be worked with in segments. The social scientist will be skeptical about how the models are used, and the biblical exegete will be skeptical about the very broad generalizations without adequate grounding in the texts. But the helpfulness of the book lies in the new insights and possibilities for interpretation provided by its cross-disciplinary method.

Applying the Models

Recently several books have appeared that have taken one or more of these social science models and read a complete biblical work or author from that perspective. They serve as examples of what can be done using social science models.

Jerome Neyrey's *An Ideology of Revolt: John's Christology in Social-Science Perspective* examines the christology of the fourth gospel first from traditional exegetical method, highlighting the gospel's claims to Jesus' equality with God and the transcendent heavenly outlook from which the world and unbelievers are judged. The second part builds primarily on Douglas' group/grid schema and her assumption that theology replicates social experience, that is, that there is an integral relationship between a group's perception of its place in the world and its understanding of God. With these tools, Neyrey sets out to locate the worldview of the Johannine Christians. By understanding their christologically-centered theology, we can presumably understand their social experience and their view of themselves and their world.[6]

One accepted theory of the fourth gospel's composition among Johannine scholars is that the text gives evidence of several stages of composition, each of which would reflect a significant stage in the life of its community. Building on this assumption, Neyrey posits three stages, each with its own strategy and developing attitudes that can be located according to group and grid.

The first stage is characterized by strong missionary activity on the part of a group of Jewish Christians still members of the synagogue; they urge Jews to a reformed faith that recognizes Jesus as fulfillment of the scriptures and of Judaism. Membership in the Johannine group is fluid and not well defined: boundaries of the group are porous. Their allegiance, and their perception of Jesus' identification, still lies strongly within Judaism, yet their own position is that of critique and challenge. Thus their position at this stage is strong group/low grid.

In the second stage, the claims of the Johannine group are becoming stronger and more exclusive. Jesus is the absolute and only way who replaces the major elements of Judaism, including temple and cult. Membership is becoming better defined and more tightly controlled as the stakes rise and confrontation increases. Here the Johannine community can be located in continuing strong group but with rising grid, since conflict between themselves and their group (Judaism) is sharpened.

The third stage represents the time in which the Johannine Christians have inevitably been excommunicated from the synagogue, a situation that we know from internal evidence (Jn 9:22; 12:42; 16:2). This puts them no longer in a position of reform, but of revolt against not only the Jewish authorities with their religious claims, but also against those Christians whose faith is judged to be inadequate (the so-called "apostolic Christians"). Their christological claims have hardened, as has their discouragement and pessimism about anything having to do with this world. All their expectations are now turned toward their heavenly revealer. At this point the group indicator has lowered, for they no longer feel part of a larger body that makes demands for conformity. The grid indicator, which was rising in stage two, has now fallen sharply, as expectation for anything good to come from this present life dwindles. They are now located in the quadrant of weak group/low grid.

For the reader inclined to invest enough energy in learning the group/grid schema to follow the arguments, such an exposition sheds light on why and how people respond as they do, how their beliefs and their worldview coincide, and how such a situation was lived out by a community of early Christians, just as similar experiences continue to be lived out by others.

Just two years later, Neyrey turned the eye of cultural anthropology on Paul in *Paul, in Other Words: A Cultural Reading of His Letters,* this time in a book intended more for the general reader. Again the work of M. Douglas provides the fundamental structures for the study, but this time some of her less complex theories from two books, *Purity and Danger* and *Natural Symbols.*[7] The format for Neyrey's book is the examination of six basic categories of worldview or symbolic universe: purity, ritual, body, sin and deviance, cosmology, and evil or misfortune.

The first chapter serves as a general introduction to anthropological thinking. In the second and third, Neyrey takes up the categories of purity and pollution in the way proposed by Douglas. Leaving aside knowledge of infection through germs, viruses, and bacteria (ideas unknown in Paul's world), pollution or in more common language dirt is simply matter out of place. Purity therefore consists of a culturally constructed system for assuring that matter stays in its socially designated place (see further the discussion of clean and unclean in chapter 2, above).

The Jewish concern for ritual purity and the Greek concern for cosmic harmony are both relevant here, and are strongly reflected in some of the ways in which Paul the Jew sees his world. Looking primarily to 1 Corinthians, Neyrey shows how Paul constructs an orderly cosmos in which people, things, time, and space are all carefully mapped out. For instance, God and people all fit into a patterned hierarchy in which the supremacy of God and Christ is matched by a human ranking from creation as well as in the church (compare 1 Cor 11:3; 12:28–30; 15:5–10). The human world is divided into believers and non-believers (1 Cor 6:6), insiders and outsiders (1 Cor 5:12–13), the holy and the unjustified (1 Cor 6:1–2).

On classification of things, see for instance the priority of prophecy over tongues in 1 Corinthians 14, or of celibacy over marriage in 1 Corinthians 7. The map of time is dominated by the watershed event of Christ's death and resurrection, which marks the difference between then and now. The map of space in Paul's writings is the most difficult to see because for him, unlike for most Jews of his time, the center was no longer the fixed geographical point of the Jerusalem temple. While continuing to worship in the temple when he visited Jerusalem, Paul nevertheless transfered the notion of sacred space to the community assembly, wherever that might take place. Thus the category of sacred space is the most fluid of the four areas for Paul. Even so, that mobile space had clear human boundaries on the question of membership.

God, however, has upset Paul's ordered universe by calling all, insiders or outsiders (Jews or Greeks), to the same salvation in Christ, acting against the human honor system by choosing what is weak and shameful (1 Cor 1:27–28). As a result, the mapping of both persons and things is upset, as law and freedom function in a new way (1 Cor 12:13; Gal 3:28). Dietary laws that require a sense of sacred time and space are upset, and reversal becomes a new but increasingly familiar pattern as old values give way to new.

The fourth chapter explores the world of rituals (transition markers) and ceremonies (reinforcement markers) in the Pauline churches. The familiar Jewish entrance ritual of circumcision is no longer acceptable for Paul; baptism takes its place. Judgment and excommunication are two kinds of exit rituals from the sacred space of the church. Together these two kinds of rituals mark off the church's boundaries.

The fifth chapter examines perceptions of the body as image of society. Where purity concerns about bodily control are high, similar concerns about the purity of the collective body will be also. The release of bodily control in ritual expresses the need for release of social control. Tight control of bodily orifices reflects tight social control, etc. Neyrey gives a very informative summary of Douglas' ideas on this theme and applies them to biblical thinking and to 1 Corinthians in particular. When some of the difficult discussions about behavior in that epistle are seen from this perspective, some very new insights can emerge, e.g. what Paul is really after in his discussion of marriage and celibacy in 1 Corinthians 7, the eating of food offered to idols in chapters 8 and 10, the questions of head covering and behavior at the Lord's supper in chapter 11, and control of the mouth when exercising the gifts of tongues and prophecy in chapters 12—14. This longest and most interesting chapter of Neyrey's book yields many informative gems.

Chapters 6, 7, and 8 deal with sin, cosmology, and suffering in Paul's worldview. Sin is seen under two different metaphors: rule breaking or corruption and disease. The dualistic cosmology of the ancient Greco-Roman world is expressed by Paul as a war between the spiritual powers of good and evil, formulated in Christian life in such dichotomies as light/darkness, spirit/flesh, blessing/curse, freedom/slavery. Jesus' war with Satan, described in the gospels, continues in the lives of his followers. The attitude toward suffering and misfortune is therefore one of personal causality. The question asked is: Who did this to me? Answer: either God in just judgment or Satan in unjust persecution.

The final two chapters of *Paul, in Other Words* study accusations of demon possession and witchcraft starting from Paul's taunt to the Galatians (Gal 3:1) and his warning about demon possession (2 Cor 11:14). Through an examination of Paul's symbolic universe as revealed specifically in Galatians and 2 Corinthians, Neyrey shows how the belief in human instrumentality and victimization in the dualistic struggle between good and evil is played out in such accusations.[8]

This extended application of the basic elements of a symbolic universe to one particular biblical writer is one of the clearest examples of what can be gained by use of the social sciences, and of cultural anthropology in particular, in biblical interpretation.

The final book that we will consider in detail is a collection of essays by nine members of *The Context Group,* a seminar formed in 1986 to pursue the application of the social sciences to biblical interpretation. While both Malina and Neyrey are members of the group and major contributors to this volume, *The Social World of Luke–Acts: Models for Interpretation* is the result of collaborative work on the part of many, a model in itself of how scholars motivated by similar interests can work together. The seminar continues to meet regularly and work on collaborative projects.

The Social World of Luke–Acts, like *Paul, in Other Words,* is written for the general reader. Chapter 1 by Malina steps back from looking at the world of the text to take a look at the act of reading, in order to alert us to the cultural and theoretical differences with which we may approach an ancient text like Luke–Acts. Chapters 2 and 3 by Malina and Neyrey are reviews of the categories of honor/shame and dyadic personality, by now familiar to readers interested in Mediterranean anthropology, but presented in completely new format from the related chapters in *The New Testament World* (see chapter 2 of the present book), and worked out with examples from Luke–Acts. Chapter 4 by Malina and Neyrey applies the labeling and deviance theory that the same authors had earlier applied to Matthew in *Calling Jesus Names*[9] to Luke–Acts, in particular to the trial of Jesus.

With chapter 5, some new authors appear with new perspectives. Here Richard Rohrbaugh gives a succinct description of the pre-industrial city and turns these findings to an analysis of the great supper (Lk 14:15–24). In the light of the operative economic and social system, so different from our modern one, the refused invitations to the banquet are not just a question of ungrateful invitees with poor manners. Rather, the story challenges the entire honor system upon which social status is built.

As complement to consideration of the city in the previous chapter, chapter 6 by Douglas Oakman studies the countryside. He points out that in spite of Luke's focus on such urban centers as Jerusalem, Antioch, and Ephesus, sixty percent of the New Testament references to country or countryside occur in Luke–Acts. After reviewing the characteristics of pre-industrial agrarian societies and their economics with special reference to peasants, he highlights those features as they appear in Luke–Acts and concludes that Luke has idealized the countryside and called for peace and justice on the terms of landowners' interests rather than those of rural peasants.

In the seventh chapter, John Pilch studies the presuppositions behind social models of sickness and healing, showing how fundamental assumptions about humanity and its relationship to nature form attitudes toward disease, illness, and healing. Within a worldview of personal causality, in which suffering and misfortune are believed to be the result of direct intervention, spirits are thought to play a significant role in health care concepts and attitudes.

Chapter 8 by John Elliott highlights the contrast between temple and household in Luke–Acts, describing the temple for Luke as a holy place that has lost its ability to make holy, a political institution that no longer represents the interests of all. By contrast, for Luke the household based on the institution of kinship, center of the house church that is the basic Christian social organization, gathers all the expectations of life according to the Spirit in God's kingdom.

Chapter 9 by Halvor Moxnes studies the patron-client relationship in Luke–Acts. The patronage system active in Greco-Roman antiquity surrounded persons of influence and prestige with social inferiors who formed with them an interlocking network of mutual alliances in which both sides act out of self-interest and thus benefit. In Luke–Acts, the patron figures, including God with Jesus and the apostles as "brokers" (representatives or mediators), do not act for their own ultimate self-interest, and thus the whole system, while retained, is radically altered.

The last four chapters of the collection by Neyrey, Vernon Robbins, and Mark McVann look at questions of symbolic universe, social location, rituals and ceremonies in Luke–Acts. This volume is the best example so far of an entire book that illustrates what can actually be done by directing social science perspective and models to a single extended biblical text. Social science models and theories are for the most part carefully grounded in the text itself. The brief summaries above do not do justice to the many valuable insights, but are meant to whet the reader's appetite for more.

In this chapter we have looked at some of the latest discussions of method and at some of the examples of what can be done with it. Social science interpretation in biblical studies is still a young method that is growing and developing rapidly. It remains to be seen where the future will lead it.

8
Prospects for the Future

New studies in social history and social description continue to appear. In this area, the methodological questions are less explicit, and therefore probably trickier. Without explicit models or theories of social interaction to guide the interpretation, the writer of social history can be less certain of seeing the world of the text in a way that somehow approximates its reception by a person contemporary to it. There is a greater risk that what seems to the modern reader the obvious meaning will be assumed to have been the obvious meaning in the first century. We have seen with the help of comparative cultural anthropology that obvious meanings are quite dependent on cultural construction.

On the other hand, the social history interpreter need not be burdened with the complexity of abstract social science models that often illuminate, but sometimes yield only the same results obtainable through more traditional methods. Sometimes, humorously enough, it seems to come down to differences in personality types: those who opt for the use of social science models tend to be those who like the big picture and are bored with details; those who opt for social description tend to be those who must have documented evidence in order to trust wider theories.

The newer and riskier method, however, is social science interpretation, which is still working out its operative canons, that is, what methods and models are useful and how they can be used. In the rest of this chapter we will consider some of the exciting challenges and potential pitfalls of the use of social science method in New Testament interpretation.

Understanding What Models Can and Cannot Do

A social science model is simply an abstract and simplified representation of how some form of social interaction works. To be valid, it should be verifiable at the same level of abstraction across a range of situations or cultures that share some of the same characteristics. It should provide some measure of predictability about how the particular aspect of the social system works.

As with any process of abstraction, however, a model of social construction and interaction must be used cautiously. It establishes a specific point of view and necessarily excludes others. It helps to break the myth of the objective observer by making us aware of at least some of the cultural presuppositions that the observer brings.

Social science models are formulated on the basis of observation of living cultures. The social science biblical interpreter attempts then to apply the same models to a situation that we can know only from a written text produced many centuries ago. This is in itself a delicate problem. Not only have we no direct access to the people who produced the texts, but there is also a great time and culture gap between them and us.

In other words, we are using models on partial glimpses of ancient cultures that were meant to be applied to whole contemporary cultures. This can only be done on the assumption that there is sufficient cultural continuity in the same place (the Mediterranean and Near East) and among the people who have continuously inhabited it. Of course, the higher the level of abstraction the more similarity will be seen; the lower the level of abstraction, the more differences will appear.

We can distinguish at least six levels of abstraction that are helpful for the biblical interpreter using the social sciences. Moving from general to more specific, the *first level* has to do with basic social institutions common to all cultures, especially kinship, economics, politics, and religion, though all four may not function independently in a given culture. It is thought, for instance, that in ancient Mediterranean society, economics was subsumed under kinship and religion, whereas in contemporary post-industrial societies, economics is often the major determinative institution in social life.

The *second level* of abstraction offers basic models of social composition and dynamics and asks according to what principles a given society operates, e.g. the three basic social theories of structural functionalism, conflict, and symbolic interaction. At the *third level* is the macrosociological classification of society—in the case of the ancient Mediterranean, a pre-industrial advanced agrarian society. At a *fourth level* is the geographical and historical entity called Mediterranean, or Mesopotamian-Mediterranean (including the Middle East), and its own fundamental value system, including such pivotal concepts as honor-shame, kinship, and purity classifications. These would be values that operate across social levels in the same culture, though they may be more stressed at one social level as compared to another. This system of semi-articulated values would include such culturally-constructed concepts as common sense, sanity, life and death.

A *fifth level* of abstraction contains models that express particular understandings of self and group within a given subgroup of that culture, including ways in which the general cultural values are integrated and reinforced at that social level. An example of this might be the ways in which early Christian groups understood themselves to be part of their world—or not part of it. Finally, a *sixth level* includes particular elements of the common worldview that are appropriated, interpreted, and modified in a special way by a subgroup. An example of this level might be the way in which slavery was interpreted in early Christianity, not by abolishing it but by attempting to humanize the relationships within the social system.

It is important that social science biblical interpreters be clear at what level they intend to operate, lest generalizations be found where they do not exist, or a model not fit because there are too many exceptions. At the appropriate level, the appropriate model should be able to confirm results attained by other interpretative methods and/or provide new insights.

Listening for the Voices of the Silenced

As we know from analysis of pre-industrial agrarian societies, only a small percentage of the population, perhaps two to three percent, constituted the urban elite in control of production, trade, and literacy. This small group and the larger group that surrounded them and catered to their needs are the most likely to leave recorded evidence of their life, while the vast majority of the population have vanished with hardly a literary trace. The tools for investigating the life of ancient non-elite populations are still in process of development. Their application to the peasant population of rural Palestine and the urban non-elite population of Greco-Roman cities greatly assists the biblical scholar's task of trying to establish the social location of Jesus, his followers, and the first Christian generations.

At every social level, and most acutely at the lower ones, half the population, the female half, is even more silent. The public-private dichotomy of ancient Mediterranean culture largely excluded women from public life except at the highest levels, and thus excluded them from history as history has been told. Every historical account told from the male point of view could be retold as seen by the women who lived through the same events, and the story would be different.

Historians are beginning to realize that sweeping generalizations about "societies" or "cultures" often apply only to the men of those cultures, that is, only to half the population. In cultures where women are confined to the private sphere or where the social world of men and that of women are sharply divided, as is still the case in many conservative Middle Eastern societies and Mediterranean peasant cultures, the social experience of women and the way their power operates are quite different. Until we give adequate attention to the social world of women in the cultures and texts we study, we will be studying only half the picture.

At present we are at the first phase of this reclaiming of the social world of women. This phase is marked by separate books, articles, and paragraphs about women in a given situation under study, e.g. in an article on religious customs, there may be a paragraph about women's participation in cult. But the fact that the aspect regarding women is singled out still means that the norm is male experience. When the task of reconstructing women's role in society has reached a more mature level, it will no longer be necessary to do special studies or sections on women, but the material will be fully integrated into the study of the culture.

Social Science Interpretation and Political Theology

Social science interpretation is really a branch of the historical critical method that has been used in biblical studies now for more than a century, in that it seeks as objective a description as possible, and uses the biblical text to gain access to the world that produced it.[1] The difference is that with its tools of critical social analysis, it has the possibility of making the interpreter aware of just how subjective any interpretation is.

After some early tentative advances toward one another,[2] social science interpretation and the various forms of political theology, especially liberation theology, have not found a comfortable alliance. Writers like the South African theologian Itumeleng Mosala warn us that social science interpretation "moves us one step forward to the extent that it focuses our attention on the social nature of our texts; but it pulls us two steps backwards" by hiding the old class interests "under the cloak of a more systematic approach."[3] Mosala asks for an open acknowledgement of the limitations of the method inasmuch as it still represents the interests of the dominant class. The tension between the social scientist's search for "objective" interpretation and the liberation theologian's forthright advocacy of positions in favor of the oppressed has yet to be effectively worked out.

The "So What?" Reaction

Those who teach the social science approach to biblical studies in a western classroom are likely to be successful at demonstrating the cultural differences that exist between us and the ancient Mediterranean people who produced the Bible. This can be very enlightening, for it shows us that we cannot simply assume that a text means what we think it means. The entire process of contextual interpretation is opened up; the problem with literal interpretation becomes evident, and students realize that meaning and interpretation are socially constructed.

For the western student, this is the deconstructive phase of the process, in which previous suppositions and certainties are torn down. Biblical texts are then approached with more suspicion, and the student is provided with some tools for ascertaining what they might have meant in their original context. But then what? The western student can be left in a theological vacuum, knowing that the old interpretive framework no longer holds, but unable to construct a new one that will provide workable interpretations for today's world. The gap between then and now has widened, and the bridge is not long enough.

For the non-western student used to a western approach, however, the reaction may be just the opposite. These texts that previously posed enormous theological problems suddenly fall into place. The reason for this discovery is that the intermediate western, post-enlightenment framework has faded away, and the non-western student finds that at a high enough level of abstraction, much of what is said about ancient Mediterranean culture is sufficiently similar to her or his original symbolic universe to create a fit. The Bible that had seemed alien because explained in western categories is now found to be home.

In both cases, but starting from different ends, a new theological task is at hand. Cultural sensitivity to each other's experience will be an important component in the reconstruction process. The social interpretation of the Bible has the potential to make a significant contribution toward intercultural and even international understanding.

Conclusion

There are many different ways to approach the New Testament. At one extreme one can be totally unconcerned about its impact on our times and be completely caught up in its historical data and its ideas as witness to the thinking of a religious sect of twenty centuries ago. At the opposite extreme one can almost completely ignore the ways in which the life described in the New Testament differs from ours, and care only about the "timeless truths" contained in it as if the meaning of the verbal expression of people in a different culture two thousand years ago could correspond exactly to that of a modern technologized culture. Obviously neither extreme is very wise.

All biblical study is located somewhere on the spectrum between these two points. The current method of social study of the New Testament makes one kind of contribution to the attempt to bridge the gap between "then" and "now" by proposing cross-cultural models of human interaction and methods for analysis of social information that can be comprehensible in a variety of social settings. Of course it must be recognized that no interpreter and no method of interpretation are completely objective, so that no matter how stringent the procedure, it is impossible to escape completely our own presuppositions and prejudices. But that is no reason to give up the attempt continually to refine the process.

In this volume we have discussed the findings of the social study of the New Testament as classified into the three major aspects of social relationship: ethnicity, status, and sex. The baptismal formula of Galatians 3:28 already expresses awareness of those divisions and the hope that, while remaining realities of life, they can in Christ cease to be divisive.

We have seen how the first Christian generations had to struggle with problems not too different from our own in the blending of cultures necessitated by the move from rural Palestinian to urban Greek environment. Within the first years after the death of Jesus his disciples were already facing the problems of cultural adaptation and ethnic differences.

Likewise the sharp social distinctions of class and status and the economic ambiguities of that world, placed in juxtaposition to an egalitarian vision that would provide a new and radical dimension to human relationships, produced another set of problems as Christianity struggled to be part of its world while yet retaining its distinctiveness.

The need to formulate structures of internal church life, and the way in which those structures impinged on the exercise of authority and freedom, posed more problems. The interrelatedness of sex roles and patterns of dominance in a heavily patriarchal society clashed with egalitarian impulses springing from the Christian vision.

Finally, we have seen how some social science models have been applied to the New Testament books with insightful results. We have also cast a glance toward the challenges and problems that face us as we face the future. The exploration of social expectations, patterns of relationship, and societal structures through the eyes of modern social science research method has its gaps and weaknesses. Its strength lies in its ability to illuminate for us not only complex patterns of behavior and relationship, but also the simple structures of everyday life upon which a society is built.

Thus the New Testament can be illuminated more closely as not only divine revelation about God, but also divine revelation to us about ourselves and the people of faith who have gone before us. We can too easily lose sight of the humanness of the scriptures because it reminds us of our frailty. The word of God can be communicated to us only in human language. The social study of the New Testament can help us better to understand that language.

Notes

Introduction

1. *The Sociology of Religion* (Beacon, 1963; original German publication, 1922); S.N. Eisenstadt, ed., *Max Weber on Charisma and Institution Building: Selected Papers* (University of Chicago, 1968).

2. *The Social Teaching of the Christian Churches,* 2 vols. (Harper, 1960; original German publication, 1912).

3. *Purity and Danger: An Analysis of Concepts of Pollution and Taboo* (Routledge and Kegan Paul, 1966); *Natural Symbols: Explorations in Cosmology* (Pantheon, 1970); "Cultural Bias" (Royal Anthropological Institute of Great Britain and Ireland, Occasional Paper 35; London: Royal Anthropological Institute, 1978), reprinted in *In the Active Voice* (Routledge and Kegan Paul, 1982), pp. 183–253.

4. *The Sacred Canopy: Elements of a Sociological Theory of Religion* (Doubleday, 1967); P. Berger and T. Luckmann, *The Social Construction of Reality: A Treatise on the Sociology of Knowledge* (Doubleday, 1966).

5. *The Ritual Process* (Aldine, 1969). For an example of use of Turner with the New Testament, see George S. Worgul, "Anthropological Consciousness and Biblical Theology," *Biblical Theology Bulletin* 9 (1979), pp. 3–12.

6. Notably: J.Z. Smith, "The Social Description of Early Christianity," *Religious Studies Review* 1 (1975), pp. 19–25; D.J. Harrington, "Social Concepts in the Early Church: A Decade of Research," *Theological Studies* 41 (1980), pp. 181–190; R. Scroggs, "The Sociological Interpretation of the New Testament: The Present State of Research," *New Testament Studies* 26 (1980), pp. 164–179; H.C. Kee, *Christian Origins in Sociological Perspective: Methods and Resources* (Westminster, 1980). Two less technical articles appeared in *Interpretation* 37:3 (July 1980): B. J. Malina, "The Social Sciences and Biblical Interpretation," pp. 229ff. 242; J.G.

Gager, "Shall We Marry Our Enemies? Sociology and the New Testament," pp. 256–265; D. Tidball, *The Social Context of the New Testament: A Sociological Analysis* (Zondervan, 1984); C. Osiek, "The New Handmaid: The Bible and the Social Sciences," *Theological Studies* 50 (1989), pp. 260–278; B. Holmberg, *Sociology of the New Testament: An Appraisal* (Fortress, 1990); P. van Staden and A.G. van Aarde, "Social Description or Social-Scientific Interpretation? A Survey of Modern Scholarship," *Hervormde Teologiese Studies* (Pretoria) 47 (1991), pp. 55–87.

Chapter 1

1. For recent up-to-date material on archaeological evidence for Herodian Jerusalem, both abundantly illustrated, see R. Mackowski, *Jerusalem, City of Jesus* (Eerdmans, 1980) and J. Wilkinson, *Jerusalem as Jesus Knew It: Archeology as Evidence* (Thames and Hudson, 1978). A thorough scholarly study of the history of Caesarea is *Caesarea Under Roman Rule* by L.J. Levine (Studies in Judaism in Late Antiquity 7; Brill, 1975). The results of the past ten years of archaeological work at Caesarea are attractively described and illustrated by R.J. Bull, "Caesarea Maritima—The Search for Herod's City" and R.L. Hohlfelder, "Caesarea Beneath the Sea," both in *Biblical Archaeology Review* 8;3 (May/June 1982), pp. 24–47; K.G. Holum, *et al.*, *King Herod's Dream: Caesarea on the Sea* (W.W. Norton, 1988).

2. M. Hengel, *Judaism and Hellenism*, Vol. 1, pp. 107–175.

3. *Ibid.*, pp. 243–247.

4. For the stories of Sepphoris and Tiberias, see Freyne, *Galilee*, pp. 122–134.

5. Freyne, *Galilee*, pp. 138–145.

6. Pp. 85–109.

7. See J.H. Leon, *The Jews of Ancient Rome* (Jewish Publication Society of America, 1960).

8. For a clear, straightforward introduction to Philo, see S. Sandmel, *Philo of Alexandria: An Introduction* (Oxford University, 1979).

9. For a more developed discussion of the main lines of these points, see Hengel, *Jews, Greeks, and Barbarians*, pp. 51–82.

Chapter 2

1. See for instance A.R. Hands, *Charities and Social Aid in Greece and Rome* (Cornell University, 1968), especially pp. 26–61.

2. *Time*, July 19, 1982, pp. 21–22.

3. "The Apostle Paul and the Introspective Conscience of the West," *Harvard Theological Review* 56 (1963), pp. 199–215; reprinted in *Paul Among Jews and Gentiles* (Fortress, 1976).

4. See Malina, *The New Testament World,* pp. 62–67 for numerous examples.

5. For archaeological evidence of small farming in the neighborhood of ancient Jerusalem, see "Ancient Jerusalem's Rural Food Basket," by G. Edelstein and S. Gibson, *Biblical Archaeology Review* 8:4 (July/August 1982), pp. 46–54.

6. A good collection of texts on the mystery religions with brief but good introductions is M.W. Meyer, ed., *The Ancient Mysteries: A Sourcebook* (Harper & Row, 1987).

7. For further thoughts by the same author, see B. Malina, "Dealing with Biblical (Mediterranean) Characters: A Guide for U.S. Consumers," *Biblical Theology Bulletin* 19:4 (1989), pp. 127–141.

Chapter 3

1. Freyne, *Galilee,* pp. 194–200. Another study of Palestinian groups from the historical sources is R.A. Horsley and John S. Hanson, *Bandits, Prophets, and Messiahs: Popular Movements at the Time of Jesus* (Winston, 1985). A study that uses historical and archaeological information as well as economic anthropology to see the gospel parables from a peasant's point of view is D. Oakman, *Jesus and the Economic Questions of His Day* (Edwin Mellen, 1986). See also C. Osiek, "Jesus and Money, or—Did Jesus Live in a Capitalist Society?" *Chicago Studies* 30:1 (1991), pp. 17–28.

2. Gerhard Lenski, *Power and Privilege: A Theory of Social Stratification* (McGraw-Hill, 1966). Another book that has been extremely influential but is difficult to obtain is T.F. Carney, *The Shape of the Past: Models and Antiquity* (Coronado, 1975).

3. Especially P. Worsley, *The Trumpet Shall Sound. A Study of "Cargo" Cults in Melanesia* (Schocken, 1968), and K. Burridge, *New Heaven, New Earth: A Study of Millenarian Activities* (Schocken, 1969). As Gager notices, both titles are inspired by New Testament apocalypticism, yet neither book deals with early Christianity.

4. *Kingdom and Community,* p. 57, n. 1.

5. As developed especially by L. Festinger, H.W. Riecken, and S. Schachter, *When Prophecy Fails: A Social and Psychological Study of a Modern Group That Predicted the Destruction of the World* (Harper and

Row, 1956), and L. Festinger, *A Theory of Cognitive Dissonance* (Stanford University, 1957).

6. German *Soziologie der Jesusbewegung* (Chr. Kaiser, 1977); English tr. by John Bowden (Fortress, 1978).

Chapter 4

1. "Peter and Paul," a CBS television production sponsored by Procter and Gamble, April 12 and 14, 1981.

2. Information about the Roman social order is readily available. A useful summary appears in Gager, *Kingdom and Community,* pp. 94–106, part of a revised version of a chapter entitled "Religion and Social Class in the Early Roman Empire" in Benko, *The Catacombs and the Colosseum,* pp. 99–120. A more extended and technical treatment is the superb chapter on "Orders and Status" in M.I. Finley, *The Ancient Economy* (U. of California, 1973), pp. 35–61. The next chapter, "Masters and Slaves," pp. 62–94, is also helpful for the present discussion.

3. Epictetus, *Discourses* 4.1.33–40, available in Loeb Classical Library, tr. by W.A. Oldfather (Harvard University, 1966), Vol. 2, pp. 253–257.

4. For further helpful discussions of these and other characteristics of Greco-Roman society, see Meeks, *The First Urban Christians,* Chapter 1, pp. 9–50.

5. For a discussion of the relationship of literary culture to social status, see A. Malherbe, *Social Aspects of Early Christianity,* pp. 29–59.

6. "Paul's Tentmaking and the Problem of His Social Class," *Journal of Biblical Literature* 97 (1978), pp. 555–564.

7. See M. Hengel, *Property and Riches in the Early Church,* Chapter 8, "The Ideal of 'Self-Sufficiency,' " pp. 54–59.

8. *Light from the Ancient East* (Baker, 1978; original German edition, 1908) and *Paul: A Study in Social and Religious History,* 2nd ed. (Harper and Row, 1957; original German edition, 1911). Many of these non-literary papyrus texts are available in *The New Testament Background: Selected Documents,* ed. C.K. Barrett (rev. ed.; Harper and Row, 1989), pp. 23–50.

9. *The Social Pattern of Christian Groups in the First Century* (Tyndale, 1960).

10. Theissen's book is actually the collection and translation of a number of essays which appeared in German in 1974 and 1975. The introduction by John H. Schütz is very helpful for background and context. In

addition, see the excellent collection of texts and historical information in *St. Paul's Corinth: Texts and Archaeology* by J. Murphy-O'Connor (Michael Glazier, 1983).

11. Theissen, *Social Setting*, p. 15, in the introduction by J. Schütz.

12. Meeks, *First Urban Christians*, p. 2.

13. The two letters preserved are probably not the only ones Paul wrote to the Corinthians (see 1 Cor 5:9), and it is generally thought by scholars that the present 2 Corinthians is an amalgamation of as many as five shorter letters. But these are literary questions which need not concern us here.

14. Theissen, *Social Setting*, p. 167.

15. A synthesis of the conclusions and main ideas of Meeks' book appears as "The Social Context of Pauline Theology" in *Interpretation* 37:3 (1982), pp. 266–277.

16. Mary Douglas, *Natural Symbols*, quoted in Meeks, *First Urban Christians*, p. 97.

Chapter 5

1. Another earlier and very helpful study on this subject is that of E. Earle Ellis, "Paul and His Co-Workers," *New Testament Studies* 20 (1974), pp. 128–144.

2. Holmberg, *Paul and Power*, p. 111; a summary of the thinking of several other authors.

3. The whole issue of charism and office is much more complicated but cannot be further pursued here. For more discussion, see Holmberg, *Paul and Power*, pp. 95–121, with innumerable further references; also John H. Schütz, *Paul and the Anatomy of Apostolic Authority* (Cambridge University, 1975); John H. Elliott, "A Catholic Gospel: Reflections on 'Early Catholicism' in the New Testament," *Catholic Biblical Quarterly* 31 (1969), pp. 213–223; Daniel J. Harrington, "The 'Early Catholic' Writings of the New Testament: The Church Adjusting to World-History," in *The Word in the World*, ed. R. Clifford and G. MacRae (Weston College Press, 1973); Carolyn Osiek, "The Relation of Charism to Rights and Duties in the New Testament Church," *The Jurist* 41 (1981), pp. 295–313, reprinted in *Official Ministry in a New Age*, ed. J. H. Provost (Permanent Seminar Studies 3; Canon Law Society of America/Catholic University, 1981), pp. 41–59.

Chapter 6

1. The topic of the role and status of women in the Greco-Roman world has been the subject of much recent research, sparked as much by

recent societal and ecclesiastical changes as by scholarly interest. For more reading, the following are especially recommended: J.P.V.D. Balsdon, *Roman Women: Their History and Habits* (John Day Co., 1963; reprint: Barnes and Noble, 1983); Mary R. Lefkowitz and Maureen B. Fant, eds., *Women's Life in Greece and Rome: A Source Book in Translation* (Johns Hopkins, 1982); Moshe Meiselman, *Jewish Woman in Jewish Law* (KTAV, 1978); Sarah B. Pomeroy, *Goddesses, Whores, Wives and Slaves: Women in Classical Antiquity* (Schocken, 1975); Leonard Swidler, *Women in Judaism* (Scarecrow, 1976); Jane F. Gardner, *Women in Roman Law and Society* (Indiana University, 1986).

2. The interpretation of 1 Peter 2:5–10 is based on the conclusions of an earlier book by Elliott, *The Elect and the Holy: An Exegetical Examination of 1 Peter 2:4–10 and the Phrase* BASILEION HIERATEUMA (royal priesthood), Supplements to *Novum Testamentum* 12 (E.J. Brill, 1966). Here he argues that the priesthood language of the passage, based chiefly on Exodus 19:6, has no association with the Israelite priesthood and temple cult, but rather refers to the special consecration of Israel, and hence the church, as God's holy people.

3. G. Theissen, *The Social Setting of Pauline Christianity*, p. 109; see further pp. 11, 37, 118, 138–139, 164.

4. Other recent examples include J. Severino Croatto, *Exodus: A Hermeneutics of Freedom* (Orbis, 1981) and Norman K. Gottwald, ed., *The Bible and Liberation: Political and Social Hermeneutics*, rev. ed. (Orbis, 1983), containing essays by Elliott, Fiorenza, Malina, Theissen, and others.

Chapter 7

1. *Knowing the Truth*, pp. 65–67.

2. See above, n. 3 of Introduction.

3. Talcott Parsons, *Politics and Social Structure* (Free Press, 1969).

4. Marshall Sahlins, *Stone Age Economics* (Aldine-Atherton, 1972), pp. 185–275.

5. Hayden White, *Metahistory: The Historical Imagination in Nineteenth Century Europe* (Johns Hopkins, 1973).

6. An earlier foundational work that takes the same approach with less explicit use of social science models is W. Meeks, "The Man from Heaven in Johannine Sectarianism," *Journal of Biblical Literature* 91 (1972), pp. 44–72.

7. See above, n. 3 of Introduction.

8. Those interested in more on witchcraft and demon possession should see B. Malina and J. Neyrey, *Calling Jesus Names: The Social Value of*

Notes

Labels in Matthew (Polebridge, 1988). The table of comparative U.S. and Mediterranean values at the end (pp. 145–151) is of special value because it is not specific to the topic of the book but is generally applicable.

9. See previous note.

Chapter 8

1. Readers not familiar with the various contemporary methods of biblical interpretation are referred to one of the following, or to any introduction to biblical interpretation: Daniel J. Harrington, *Interpreting the New Testament: A Practical Guide* (Michael Glazier, 1979); Terence J. Keegan, *Interpreting the Bible: A Popular Introduction to Biblical Hermeneutics* (Paulist, 1985).

2. See chapter 6, n. 4; also Christopher Rowland and Mark Corner, *Liberating Exegesis: The Challenge of Liberation Theology to Biblical Studies* (Westminster/John Knox, 1989).

3. Itumeleng Mosala, *Biblical Hermeneutics and Black Theology in South Africa* (Eerdmans, 1989), pp. 57–58, 65.

Suggestions for Further Study

Balch, David L. *Let Wives Be Submissive: The Domestic Code in 1 Peter.*
Society of Biblical Literature: Scholars Press, 1981. A fascinating
historical, literary, and social study of the origins of the household
code and its function in 1 Peter.

Benko, Stephen and John J. O'Rourke. *The Catacombs and the Colosseum: The Roman Empire as the Setting of Primitive Christianity.*
Valley Forge, PA: Judson, 1971. A helpful collection of studies on
various social aspects of life in the early Roman empire and how they
may have influenced early Christianity.

Bruce, F.F. *New Testament History.* New York: Doubleday, 1971. An excellent summary of the historical background to the New Testament that
is solid but not too heavy.

Elliott, John H. *A Home for the Homeless: A Sociological Exegesis of 1
Peter. Its Situation and Strategy.* Minneapolis: Fortress. Rev. ed.,
1991. A study of the place and function of 1 Peter in the early church
and its intended solutions to specific social problems of Christian
conversion, done through exegesis and sociological theory. The revised edition (original, 1981) contains a good survey of recent work in
social-science interpretation.

Fiorenza, Elisabeth Schüssler. *In Memory of Her: A Feminist Theological
Reconstruction of Christian Origins.* New York: Crossroad, 1983. In
spite of the title, neither exclusively feminist nor exclusively theological, but rather a bold new attempt to blend exegesis, sociology, history and theology in retelling the story of Christian origins from a
feminist perspective.

Freyne, Sean. *Galilee from Alexander the Great to Hadrian, 323 B.C.E. to
135 C.E.: A Study of Second Temple Judaism.* Wilmington: Michael
Glazier, and Notre Dame: University of Notre Dame, 1980. Extensively documented, scholarly study of the social and economic life of

Galilee in New Testament times. A shorter sequel, *Galilee, Jesus, and the Gospels: Literary Approaches and Historical Investigations* (Philadelphia: Fortress, 1988), grounds the analysis more firmly in the literary world of the synoptic gospels.

Freyne, Sean. *The World of the New Testament*. New Testament Message 2; Wilmington: Michael Glazier, 1980. A good combination of historical, political, and social data in popular form.

Gager, John G. *Kingdom and Community: The Social World of Early Christianity*. Englewood Cliffs: Prentice-Hall, 1975. One of the first serious attempts to apply sociological theory to early Christianity.

Grant, Robert M. *Early Christianity and Society*. San Francisco: Harper and Row, 1977. Seven enlightening essays on cultural and economic aspects of the Roman world and what we know of Christians' part in them.

Hengel, Martin. *Judaism and Hellenism*. 2 vols. Philadelphia: Fortress, 1974. Extensive, detailed, scholarly, ground-breaking analysis of the influence of Greek civilization on Palestine. *Jews, Greeks, and Barbarians: Aspects of the Hellenization of Judaism in the Pre-Christian Period*. Philadelphia: Fortress, 1980; *The "Hellenization" of Judaea in the First Centuries after Christ*. Philadelphia: Trinity Press International, 1990. Much smaller but no less thorough continuations of *Judaism and Hellenism* with further insights and some extension to the diaspora.

Hengel, Martin. *Property and Riches in the Early Church: Aspects of a Social History of Early Christianity*. Philadelphia: Fortress, 1974. A brief, clearly-written study of the early Christian attitude toward wealth, with contemporary problems very much in mind.

Hock, Ronald R. *The Social Context of Paul's Ministry: Tentmaking and Apostleship*. Philadelphia: Fortress, 1980. A brief and interesting investigation of the social context of Paul's trade and his insistence on refusing support from most of the communities which he founded.

Holmberg, Bengt. *Paul and Power: The Structure of Authority in the Primitive Church as Reflected in the Pauline Epistles*. Philadelphia: Fortress, 1980. A tightly-knit historical and sociological investigation of patterns of authority in the first generation of Christian missionaries.

Holmberg, Bengt. *Sociology and the New Testament: An Appraisal*. Minneapolis: Fortress, 1990. A clear survey of studies that interact with sociology, expressly excluding anthropology, with more coverage of European scholars than is done by American authors in the field.

Horsley, Richard A. *Sociology and the Jesus Movement*. New York: Crossroad, 1989. A scathing attack on the methodological inadequacy of

Theissen's *Sociology of Early Palestinian Christianity* that goes on to use the social stratification model of G. Lenski to reconstruct an image of early first century Palestine that gives more importance to social tensions than the implicit functionalism used by Theissen.

Kee, Howard C. *Christian Origins in Sociological Perspective: Methods and Resources.* Philadelphia: Westminster, 1980. An inclusive summary treatment, with ample documentation, of the major categories helpful for a sociological interpretation of the New Testament: worldview, leadership and authority, identity, the role of religion and culture, the social function of the New Testament writings themselves.

Kee, Howard C. *Knowing the Truth: A Sociological Approach to New Testament Interpretation.* Minneapolis: Fortress, 1989. This exploration of method seeks more to generate the models directly from the texts themselves rather than from social theory.

Malherbe, Abraham J. *Social Aspects of Early Christianity.* Second Edition. Philadelphia: Fortress, 1983. Several pithy essays on the social background and its possible influences on early Christian educational and ecclesial life.

Malina, Bruce J. *Christian Origins and Cultural Anthropology: Practical Models for Biblical Interpretation.* Atlanta: John Knox, 1986. An extended workbook for using a variety of social-science models with New Testament texts.

Malina, Bruce J. *The New Testament World: Insights from Cultural Anthropology.* Atlanta: John Knox, 1981. Remarkably lucid explanation of some major anthropological insights applied to the biblical world. Very readable, intended for college students.

Malina, Bruce J. and Jerome H. Neyrey. *Calling Jesus Names: The Social Value of Labels in Matthew.* Sonoma: Polebridge, 1988. A study of labeling and accusations, primarily directed against Jesus, in Matthew, seen from the perspective of deviance theory. An appendix comparing U.S. and Mediterranean cultural values is especially valuable.

Malina, Bruce and Richard Rohrbaugh. *Social-Science Commentary on the Synoptic Gospels.* Minneapolis: Fortress, 1992. Background descriptions of ancient Mediterranean life as immediately applicable to synoptic gospels, arranged sequentially. A handy reference guide to social implications of specific synoptic texts.

Meeks, Wayne. *The First Urban Christians: The Social World of the Apostle Paul.* New Haven and London: Yale University, 1983. A massively detailed investigation of the urban world, social status and internal life of the Pauline communities, exhaustively documented yet primarily intended for the general but serious reader.

Moxnes, Halvor. *The Economy of the Kingdom: Social Conflict and Economic Relations in Luke's Gospel.* Minneapolis; Fortress, 1988. An examination of the economics and theology of Luke from the perspective of macrosociological analysis of first century society.

Neyrey, Jerome. *An Ideology of Revolt: John's Christology in Social-Science Perspective.* Philadelphia: Fortress, 1988. An interesting and thorough (but not simple) study of John using the group/grid model of Mary Douglas.

Neyrey, Jerome. *Paul, in Other Words: A Cultural Reading of His Letters.* Louisville: Westminster/John Knox, 1990. An interesting and readable study of some key Pauline passages through the lens of the anthropological category of purity concerns.

Neyrey, Jerome, ed. *The Social World of Luke–Acts: Models for Interpretation.* Peabody: Hendrickson, 1991. For those who want to learn how to work with a biblical text using a variety of social-science models, this collection of essays is an excellent example.

Oakman, Douglas E. *Jesus and the Economic Questions of His Day.* Studies in the Bible and Early Christianity 8. Lewiston/Queenston: Edwin Mellen, 1986. A painstaking study that combines information from the gospels with macrosociology and economics to produce a picture of the economic circumstances of first century Palestine.

Peterson, Norman R. *Rediscovering Paul: Philemon and the Sociology of Paul's Narrative World.* Philadelphia: Fortress, 1985. A combination of sociology of knowledge and narrative criticism that wrests from this brief epistle a surprising amount of information.

Pilch, John J. *Introducing the Cultural Context of the New Testament.* Vol. 2. (See also *Introducing the Cultural Context of the Old Testament,* Vol. 1.) Mahwah: Paulist, 1992. Basic and helpful introductions to reading the Bible cross-culturally.

Reicke, Bo. *The New Testament Era: The World of the Bible from 500 B.C. to A.D. 100.* Philadelphia: Fortress, 1968. Extensive historical and political background in readable style and manageable length.

Saldarini, Anthony J. *Pharisees, Scribes and Sadducees in Palestinian Society: A Sociological Approach.* The gospels and Josephus are highlighted by Gerhard Lenski's macrosociology of advanced agrarian societies to suggest a social location for the opponents of Jesus.

Theissen, Gerd. *The Social Setting of Pauline Christianity: Essays on Corinth.* Translation and introduction by John Schütz. Philadelphia: Fortress, 1982. Collected translations of several key articles first published in German, providing new social perspectives on composition and tensions of the Corinthian community.

Theissen, Gerd. *The Sociology of Early Palestinian Christianity.* Philadelphia: Fortress, 1978. Systematic study of the social structures and functions of the first Christians in Palestine in the years closest to the time of Jesus.

Tidball, Derek. *The Social Context of the New Testament: A Sociological Analysis.* Grand Rapids: Zondervan, 1984. Another helpful survey of recent work in the area of sociological exegesis.

Verner, David C. *The Household of God: The Social World of the Pastoral Epistles.* Chico, CA: Scholars, 1983. A helpful scholarly study of the pastorals in the light of the Hellenistic household.

Other Books in this Series

What are they saying about Mysticism?
   by Harvey D. Egan, S.J.
What are they saying about Christ and World Religions?
   by Lucien Richard, O.M.I.
What are they saying about non-Christian Faith?
   by Denise Lardner Carmody
What are they saying about Christian-Jewish Relations?
   by John T. Pawlikowski
What are they saying about Creation?
   by Zachary Hayes, O.F.M.
What are they saying about the Prophets?
   by David P. Reid, SS.CC.
What are they saying about Moral Norms?
   by Richard M. Gula, S.S.
What are they saying about Sexual Morality?
   by James P. Hanigan
What are they saying about Dogma?
   by William E. Reiser, S.J.
What are they saying about Peace and War?
   by Thomas A. Shannon
What are they saying about Papal Primacy?
   by J. Michael Miller, C.S.B.
What are they saying about Matthew?
   by Donald Senior, C.P.
What are they saying about Biblical Archaeology?
   by Leslie J. Hoppe, O.F.M.
What are they saying about Scripture and Ethics?
   by William C. Spohn, S.J.
What are they saying about Theological Method?
   by J. J. Mueller, S.J.
What are they saying about Virtue?
   by Anthony J. Tambasco
What are they saying about Genetic Engineering?
   by Thomas A. Shannon
What are they saying about Paul?
   by Joseph Plevnik, S.J.